Vocabulary
Level 5
Table of Contents

Vocabulary Grade 5

INTRODUCTION

As students advance from grade to grade, word meaning becomes an important factor in comprehension since students encounter many unfamiliar words at these levels. When a student lacks a good meaning vocabulary, sentence comprehension and paragraph comprehension become difficult because of the many gaps in the continuity of the reading process.

It is important that the teacher build on the student's background of experiences as much as possible. The informational articles in this book have been selected to give the kind of direct and indirect experiences the student needs.

Throughout the book, new vocabulary words are introduced within the context of the articles. Students can use these context clues to determine the meaning of unfamiliar words. The use of context clues is often one of the easiest taught of the reading skills, and yet many students are unaware that it can be an effective method of deriving the meaning and/or pronunciation of words.

It has accurately been stated that the pen is mightier than the sword. The exercises in this book will help students make better use of their pens, and also their tongues, for they will develop their skill in using words effectively both in writing and in speaking.

ORGANIZATION

Each of the five units focuses on specific curriculum areas: Health and Learning; Geography and Weather; Science and Technology; Plants and Animals; and Sports and Hobbies. Each unit contains five informational articles. Each article introduces eight vocabulary words. Following each article are two pages of word-building activities.

A focus on the second page of each lesson is using the words in a labeling activity. Further research may be necessary for the students to complete this activity. The activity pages also contain exercises that give students practice in figuring out the meaning of words. They include solving crossword puzzles, completing analogies, classifying words, finding synonyms, and matching words and meanings. The activity pages also contain suggestions for further exploration of the topic as well as suggestions for research projects and writing assignments.

USE

Vocabulary is designed for independent use by students. Copies of the activities can be given to individuals, pairs of students, or small groups for completion. They can also be used as a center activity.

To begin, determine the implementation that fits your students' needs and your classroom structure. The following plan suggests a format for this implementation.

1. **Explain** the purpose of the activities to your class.

2. **Review** the mechanics of how you want students to work with the exercises. Do you want to introduce the subject of each article? Do you want to tap into the students' prior knowledge of the subject, and create a word web?

3. **Do** a practice activity together. Review with students how to use context to figure out the meaning of a word. Remind them to use a dictionary when the context is not enough to figure out the meaning.

4. **Determine** how you will monitor the Assessment Test and Unit Reviews. Do you want to administer them to the whole class, or to a group that has successfully completed a unit?

5. **Assure** students that all of the material is for practice purposes only. It is to help them improve their vocabulary.

ADDITIONAL NOTES

1. **Parent Communication.** Use the Parent Letter, and encourage students to share the Letter to Students with their parents. Decide if you want to keep the activity pages and unit reviews in portfolios for conferencing, or if you want students to take them home as they complete them.

2. **Bulletin Board.** Display selected research projects and writing assignments in your classroom. Encourage students to share the results of their research with classmates.

3. **Have fun.** Encourage students to create vocabulary games such as concentration and bingo that will give them practice using the vocabulary words.

Dear Parent:

A strong vocabulary is the key to success in reading and other school subjects as well as in speech and writing. Your child will be working on some practice materials to increase his or her vocabulary.

Using *Vocabulary*, we will read articles about many topics covering five themes. Vocabulary selected for study is presented in the articles. The articles are followed by activities to help your child learn word meanings and apply his or her understanding in a variety of ways. Your child may be assigned projects and writing assignments related to the topics. These assignments are planned to increase your child's vocabulary in reading, writing, and speaking.

Your child may bring home his or her folder of vocabulary activities. It is helpful if you and other family members talk about the work and share in the success of your child's achievement. Discuss the activities and the words learned. With your child, look for the words in print materials at home. Visit the library to get other books and videos on the topics the child has read and is interested in studying. This effort will encourage your child and promote learning throughout life.

Thank you for your help!

Sincerely,

Dear Student:

You're about to have an adventure. You'll be amazed, surprised, and challenged. You'll read about ships in the air, creatures of the deep, and giant insects. You'll discover forests underwater and find out what makes a tornado spin. You'll read why it's important to take good care of your heart and your teeth. Along the way, you'll be introduced to a whole new vocabulary.

You will take an assessment test to show how many words you already know. Then we will begin 25 lessons that contain informational articles focusing on health and learning, geography and weather, science and technology, plants and animals, and sports and hobbies.

Each of the lessons is a one-page article with two pages of activities. The activities give you an opportunity to figure out the meanings of words, to do further research about the topic of each selection, and to apply what you have learned.

Please plan to keep all your lessons in a notebook or folder. You may want to decorate the folder! When you have done each unit, you will get to show how much you have learned. In order to help you remember the vocabulary words, please get in the habit of using them in your writings and in your speech.

Have fun as you begin this adventure. Plan to work hard and to learn everything you can—not only about the words, but also about the topics!

Sincerely,

Assessment Test

Replace the word or words in bold type with a vocabulary word. Circle the vocabulary word. Read the sentence again to check your answer.

1. After a few weeks, the family began to feel **at ease** in their new home.

   endangered   protective   comfortable

2. The cars **crashed against each other** at the intersection.

   collided   maintained   contracted

3. The writer **changed in order to make suitable** his play for television.

   inverted   adapted   evolved

4. I had to **release air from** the tires on my bicycle.

   deflate   inflate   damage

5. Road crews **keep in a desirable condition** our highways.

   maintain   holdfast   contract

6. A tiger is **an animal that lives by preying on other animals.**

   a probe   a canine   a predator

7. Worms and clams are **animals without backbones.**

   portable   invertebrates   topographic

Assessment Test

8. Our teacher is **dividing and giving out in portions** new books to us.

   accessing   distributing   engraving

9. A high fever can be **a sign or indication** of an infection.

   a catalog   an image   a symptom

10. The announcer read a **brief account that contains the main points** of the day's news.

    summary   range   factor

Read each meaning. Fill in the bubble beside the word that fits the meaning.

11. an animal that lives on or in another animal
    ○ sucker
    ○ parasite
    ○ entomologist

12. a group of animals or plants of the same kind that live together
    ○ colony
    ○ funnel
    ○ habitat

13. left without cover or protection
    ○ damaged
    ○ exposed
    ○ dissolved

14. a hard substance formed by the skeletons of tiny sea animals
    ○ pulp
    ○ stipe
    ○ coral

Assessment Test

15. a special job or task
- ⃝ mission
- ⃝ tournament
- ⃝ specimen

16. newly hatched forms of some insects
- ⃝ valves
- ⃝ spasms
- ⃝ larvae

17. small ships used for pleasure trips
- ⃝ booms
- ⃝ yachts
- ⃝ chambers

18. quickness and ease in moving or thinking
- ⃝ stamina
- ⃝ mantle
- ⃝ agility

19. the part of the body that lies between the chest and the hips
- ⃝ abdomen
- ⃝ epicenter
- ⃝ organism

20. a list of items
- ⃝ range
- ⃝ catalog
- ⃝ vortex

21. structures that control the flow of blood from the heart
- ⃝ valves
- ⃝ tentacles
- ⃝ suckers

22. a contest in which a number of competitors take part
- ⃝ tsunami
- ⃝ platform
- ⃝ tournament

23. aware; able to respond
- ⃝ comfortable
- ⃝ conscious
- ⃝ protective

24. the right to use
- ⃝ access
- ⃝ detect
- ⃝ siphon

25. the ability to learn and remember things
- ⃝ agility
- ⃝ qualified
- ⃝ intelligence

Name _____ Date _____

Watch Out for Weather!

Read this information about health risks related to the weather. Think about the meanings of the words in bold type.

Like everyone else, you spend a lot of time playing outdoors. You may participate in a team sport, like baseball, football, basketball, or hockey. You may enjoy skiing, ice skating, swimming, biking, or hiking. All of these activities improve your health and fitness, but they also can be risky. You can sprain an ankle, pull a muscle, scrape a knee, or even injure your head. You can also have problems that are due to changes in the weather.

If you play hard on a hot summer day, you could suffer from **heat exhaustion**. What are the **symptoms**? The first signs that your body is having trouble dealing with the heat are painful muscle **spasms** in the legs and **abdomen**. You may also feel weak, dizzy, or have a headache. Your skin will be cold and clammy, and you'll begin to sweat. As a result, your body loses a lot of water and salt. What should you do? First find a cool, shady spot and lie down. Drink liquids in small amounts. You can prevent heat exhaustion by drinking a lot of fluids before you go out to play and while you are playing.

Hot temperatures can cause problems, but so can cold weather. If you are out playing on a bitterly cold day or fall into icy water, you could experience **hypothermia**. The first symptom of hypothermia is shivering. If you can't get to a warm place, your body temperature will drop and your **pulse** rate will slow. Your muscles will turn **rigid**, and you may lose consciousness.

What can you do to help someone who is suffering from hypothermia? If the person is unconscious, you must get him to a hospital immediately. If the person is **conscious**, wrap him with coats or blankets and give him warm liquids. As with heat exhaustion, you can take steps to prevent hypothermia. On cold days, wear several layers of clothing and a hat. A hat is important because you lose most of your body heat through an uncovered head.

Focus on Safety

Edit   **Create**   **Identify**

Label
Classify
Order

Label the drawing with the correct vocabulary words.

"I think you're suffering from
3. _____."

symptoms

conscious

pulse   hypothermia

rigid

heat exhaustion

spasms

abdomen

"I'm having muscle
1. _____
in my legs and
2. _____."

"Your
4. _____ rate is slow. That's one of the 5. _____ of
6. _____."

Also...

1. Find an antonym for *rigid*.
2. Find a synonym for *conscious*.

Research   **Apply**   **Process**

Maps
Graphs
Charts

Complete the chart
with the correct
vocabulary words.

symptoms

pulse

heat exhaustion

conscious

hypothermia

spasms

rigid

abdomen

Recognize the Signs

_____	
_____	_____
1. muscle _____	1. shivering _____
2. dizziness, weakness	2. slow _____ rate
3. sweating	3. _____ muscles

U

D

L   R

Learn the Vocabulary

Create a dictionary of medical terms. Write each word on a separate sheet of
paper. Write a definition for each word. Provide illustrations where necessary.
Be sure to include the words *conscious* and *abdomen* in your dictionary.

U

D

L   R

The Beat Goes On!

Read this information about the heart. Think about the meanings of the words in bold type.

Inside your chest is a muscle in your body that began working seven months before you were born. It will never stop working as long as you live. This muscle, no larger than a man's fist, is a masterpiece of design. It is the heart.

The heart is a powerful organ. The walls are made of a special muscle called the **cardiac muscle**. Cardiac muscle is **involuntary** because it works without your thinking about it. Look at the diagram. Notice that the wall of muscle goes right through the middle of the heart, dividing it in half. Each half, or side, has two compartments. The top compartment is called the **atrium** and the bottom compartment is called the **ventricle**. You will also see **valves**. Valves stop the blood from going back the way it came.

When blood enters the atria (plural form of *atrium*), they **contract**, or squeeze tight. This forces blood through the valves down into the ventricles. When the ventricles are full, they contract. This pumps blood out to the lungs and the rest of the body. Place your hand over your heart. The beating is caused by the ventricles squeezing blood into the **aorta**, the main artery.

At birth your heart beats about 140 times a minute, but it slows down as you get older. Right now your heart beats about 80 to 100 times a minute. When you are grown, your heart will beat between 70 and 90 times a minute.

Each day the heart pumps about 17 tons of blood through thousands of miles of pipeline. The pipeline consists of the veins, arteries, and capillaries that form a web through your body. If you could take all these **blood vessels** and place them end to end, they would reach about 60,000 miles! Yet, for a drop of blood to make its tour through the body and back to the heart takes less than one minute! Your heart is, indeed, a powerful pump. It's what keeps you alive!

Edit **Create** **Identify**

Label
Estimate
Label

Label the drawing with the correct vocabulary words. You will write some words twice.

— In a Heartbeat —

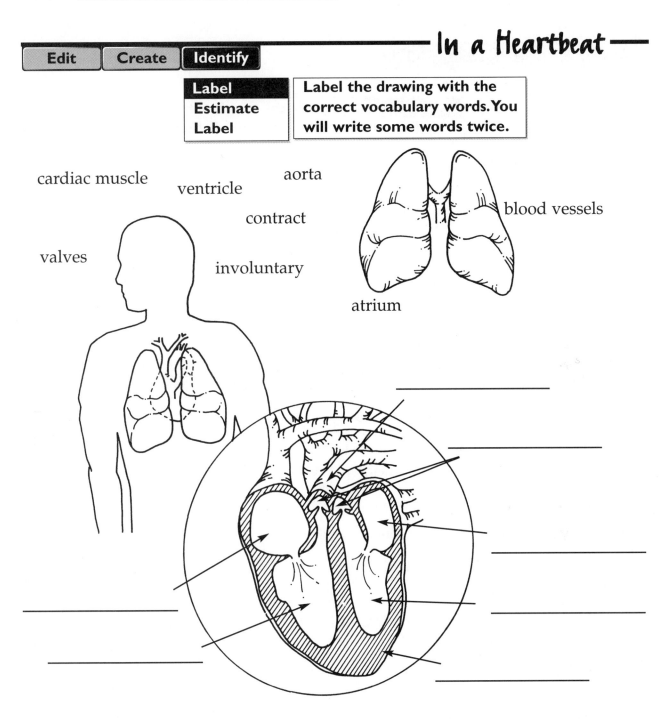

cardiac muscle

ventricle

aorta

contract

valves

involuntary

blood vessels

atrium

Also...

1. Name some *involuntary* actions, like sneezing.
2. Use a balloon to demonstrate the meaning of *contract*.
3. Name the three kinds of *blood vessels* in the human body.

Name _____   Date _____

Classify
Identify
Match

Identify the vocabulary word that fits each clue.

atrium

aorta

blood vessels

valves   contract

involuntary

ventricle

cardiac muscle

Taking Your Pulse

1. The blood circulates through these.   _____

2. A thing gets smaller when it does this.   _____

3. This is the top section of your heart.   _____

4. This is the bottom section of your heart.   _____

5. These control the flow of blood.   _____

6. This is the main artery of your body.   _____

7. This is not done on purpose.   _____

8. The wall of your heart is made of this.   _____

Be a Cardiac Specialist

Create a model of the heart from modeling clay. Use the model to describe the organ and how it works. Be sure to use as many vocabulary words as you can in your explanation.

Teeth—The Inside Story

Read this information about caring for your teeth. Think about the meanings of the words in bold type.

Teeth are very important. Without them, you would not be able to chew food. If you look at your teeth in a mirror, you'll find that they can be divided into three main groups. At the front are eight chisel-shaped teeth called **incisors** that you use to bite your food. After the incisors come the four pointed tearing teeth called **canines**. At the very back are the grinding specialists—large, broad teeth with a number of points or cusps. These are the **molars**. Between the canines and the molars are the **premolars** or bicuspids that crush your food.

The white part that you can see above the gum is called the **crown**. The crown is covered with enamel, the hardest substance in your body. Under the enamel is a layer of a bonelike substance called **dentin**. In the center of the tooth is a soft **pulp** that contains nerves and blood vessels. The part that fits into a hole in the jawbone is its **root**.

You get two sets of teeth in a lifetime. First to appear is a set of 20 milk teeth. One by one, your milk teeth loosen and fall out and permanent teeth grow in their place. By the age of about 21, you will have 32 of these teeth. There are no replacements for these teeth.

Food left on your teeth attracts a coating of germs called plaque. Most plaque grows between the teeth and at the edges of the gums. The germs in the plaque make acid as they feed on bits of food in the mouth. The acid attacks the enamel and starts to eat into the tooth, which causes tooth decay. If the decay goes through to the pulp, you will get a toothache. Plaque may also cause gum disease. To avoid tooth decay and gum disease, brush and floss your teeth after each meal and visit the dentist regularly—about every six months. Remember, these are the only teeth you'll ever have!

Open Wide!

| Edit | Create | **Identify** |

| **Label** |
| Classify |
| Order |

Label the drawing with the correct vocabulary words.

incisors   root   premolars

canines   crown

pulp

molars

dentin

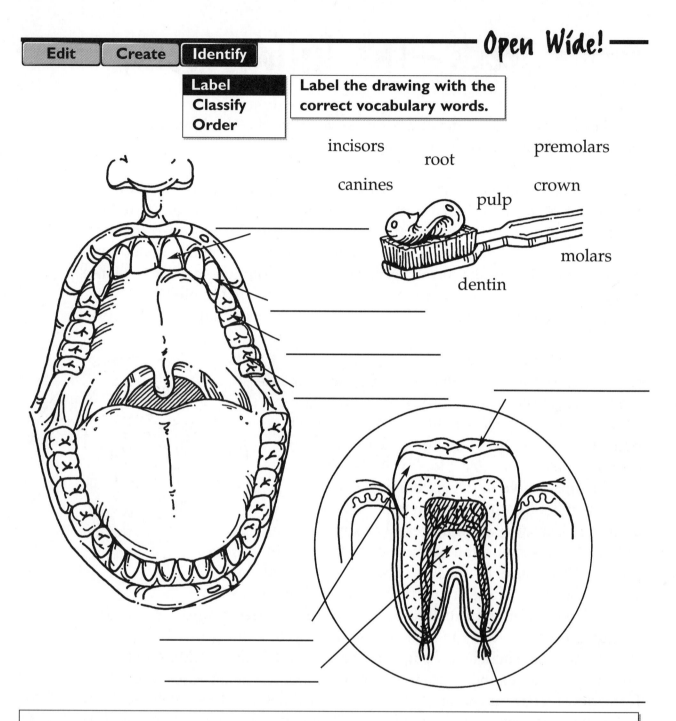

Also...

1. The word *premolars* starts with the prefix *pre-*. Find the meaning of the prefix. Think of other words that begin with this prefix.

2. The word *incisors* starts with the prefix *in-*. Find the meaning of the prefix. Think of other words that begin with this prefix.

Research   Apply   **Process**

Identify
Match
Find

Identify the vocabulary word that fits each meaning.

incisors

molars   premolars

pulp   dentin

canines

root

crown

Get Your Teeth Into This Puzzle!

the part of the tooth that can be seen above the gums

1				

teeth located between the canines and the molars

	2						

the part of the tooth beneath the enamel

				4	

the part of the tooth that connects it to the jawbone

		5	

the large teeth at the back of the mouth

3					

the soft inner part of the tooth, consisting of nerve and blood vessels

	6		

Write the numbered letters in the puzzle. You will discover the name of the bony layer that covers the outside of the root and holds the tooth in place.

1	2	3	2	4	5	6	3

What's That You Say?

Read this information about your ears. Think about the meanings of the words in bold type.

Everything you know about the world comes to you through your senses. You feel, taste, smell, see, and hear objects through your sense **organs**, like your tongue, nose, and eyes. Ears, of course, are the organs that collect sounds.

How are sounds made? Stretch a rubber band, then pluck it. You will see the band move up and down so fast that it becomes blurred. These shaking movements, called **vibrations**, make the sounds you hear. All sounds are made by objects vibrating.

When sound waves hit the **eardrum**—a circular tissue in the middle ear—it vibrates. Three tiny bones make the vibrations stronger and pass them on to the inner ear. The inner ear consists of a **complex** system of tubes filled with a watery liquid. Vibrations from the middle ear make the liquid move. **Sensitive** nerve endings **convert**, or change, this movement into electrical signals which the brain "hears."

Your ear does other jobs for you besides hearing. The ear measures distance and is also your body's balancing organ. You would not be able to stand up without it. It allows you to move around and know which way is up. Try these experiments to find out how important your ears are. Cover your ears with earplugs. Now walk around doing your **normal** activities. Which ones do you find difficult? Now blindfold yourself and ask a friend to lead you around a familiar room. Tap objects as you move. Try to guess where you are and what the objects are. You'll see how important your sense of hearing is.

The best thing you can do to protect your hearing is to avoid loud noises. Playing music too loudly for long periods of time can **damage** your hearing. If you can't control the noise, wear earmuffs or earplugs.

Just Listen!

| Edit | Create | **Identify** |

Label	Label the drawing with the
Classify	correct vocabulary words.
Order	

normal

complex

organs

convert

sensitive

eardrum

damage

vibrations

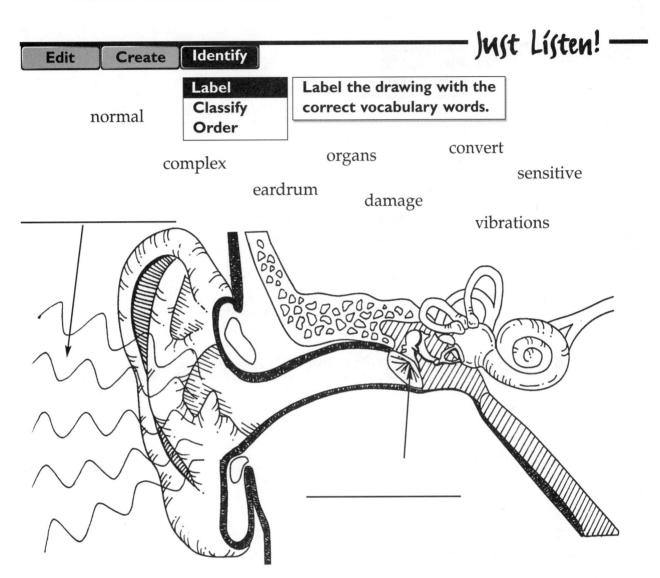

Your ear is one of your sense _____ . Its primary job

is to collect sounds from the air and _____ them into

nerve impulses which the brain "hears."

Also...

1. Find antonyms for *normal* and *damage*.
2. Find synonyms for *sensitive* and *complex*.

Research | **Apply** | **Process**

Complete
Add
Match

Complete each pair of sentences with the correct vocabulary word.

organs

sensitive

convert

normal

damage

vibrations

eardrum

complex

Put Your Ear to the Ground

1. Biceps are muscles.
   Ears are _____ .

2. The cochlea is part of the inner ear.
   The _____ is part of the middle ear.

3. An amoeba is a simple organism.
   A worm is a _____ organism.

4. Your nose detects odors.
   Your ear collects _____ from the air.

5. You can repair a bicycle with a wrench.
   You can _____ a bicycle with a sledge hammer.

U
D
L R

You're All Ears!

Draw a diagram of the inner ear. Label the *eardrum*, hammer, anvil, stirrup, and cochlea. Then explain how the ear functions. Use the words *sensitive*, *convert*, and *normal* in your explanation.

U
D
L R

Name _____   Date _____

Finding Books in a Library

Read this information about using a library's catalog. Think about the meanings of the words in bold type.

Suppose you wanted to find a library book about the giant octopus, coral reefs, or dirigibles. You can **locate** almost any book quickly and easily by using a card **catalog**. For every book in the library, the card catalog contains an **author card** and a **title card**. In addition, a third card—a **subject card**—is included for each nonfiction book and for many fiction books.

On the top line of the author card, you will see the author's name, with the last name first. Below it, other information is given, such as its title, the location and name of the **publisher**, year of publication, number of pages, and a brief **summary** of the contents. The author card is filed alphabetically.

On the title card, the title of the book is given on the top line. The information that follows it is the same as that on the author card. A title card is filed alphabetically by the first word in the title unless that word is *A*, *An*, or *The*, in which case the second word in the title is used for filing.

The top line of a subject card tells the subject of the book, or what the book is about. Information below the top line is the same as that on the author card.

Today, you can **access** the catalog by using a personal computer at the library or at your home or school. To search for an author, press the <Author Search> key. Then type the name of the author (last name first) and press <Return>. To search for a title, press the <Title Search> key. Type your title and press <Return>. To find books on a particular subject, press the <Subject Search> key. Type your subject and press <Return>.

363.12	Tanaka, Shelley
TAN	The disaster of the Hindenburg, by Shelley Tanaka. New York, Scholastic/Madison Press Book, 1993. 64 p. illus.
	Describes the last voyage of the zeppelin, or airship, Hindenburg, which crashed in flames on a New Jersey airfield.

The Search Goes On!

| Edit | Create | Identify |

locate

subject card

author card   catalog

| Label |
| Estimate |
| Match |

Label the cards with the correct vocabulary words.

access   title card

publisher   summary

363.12   **Tanaka, Shelley**
TAN   The disaster of the Hindenburg, by Shelley Tanaka. New York,
Scholastic/Madison Press Book, 1993.
          64 p. illus.

          Describes the last voyage of the zeppelin, or airship, Hindenburg,
          which crashed in flames on a New Jersey airfield.

363.12   **The disaster of the Hindenburg**
TAN   **Tanaka, Shelley**
               The disaster of the Hindenburg, by Shelley Tanaka. New York,
Scholastic/Madison Press Book, 1993.
          64 p. illus.

          Describes the last voyage of the zeppelin, or airship, Hindenburg,
          which crashed in flames on a New Jersey airfield.

363.12   **AIRSHIPS**
TAN   **Tanaka, Shelley**
               The disaster of the Hindenburg, by Shelley Tanaka. New York,
Scholastic/Madison Press Book, 1993.
          64 p. illus.

          Describes the last voyage of the zeppelin, or airship, Hindenburg,
          which crashed in flames on a New Jersey airfield.

Also...

1. Find an antonym for *locate*.
2. Find a synonym for *access*.

3. Find the alternate spelling of *catalog*.

Research   **Apply**   **Process**

| Replace |
| Classify |
| Define |

Replace the word or words in bold type with a vocabulary word.

locate

access

subject card

title card

publisher

author card

catalog

summary

Quiet, Please!

1. How can you **find** a book in the school or public library?   _____

2. Almost every library has a **list of items**.   _____

3. Each card has information about the book, such as the name of the **company that printed the book**.   _____

4. The card also has a **brief account that contains the main points** of the book.   _____

5. You can also **approach** the information with a personal computer.   _____

On Your Own

Think of a topic you want to research. Use the library catalog to find books that have information about the topic. Copy an *author card* for one book, a *title card* for another book, and a *subject card* for a third book on your list.

Unit 1 Review

Antonyms are words that have opposite or nearly opposite meanings. Read these sentences. Circle the antonym for each word in bold type.

rigid   1. My schedule is flexible, so come whenever you can.

contracts   2. Metal expands when it is heated.

root   3. The crown of the tooth can be seen above the gums.

normal   4. It's unusual for him not to want to go to a soccer game.

locate   5. When did you lose your spelling book?

conscious   6. The deer were unaware of my presence.

involuntary   7. Her actions were intentional.

complex   8. Learning to ride a bicycle is not so simple.

sensitive   9. Her uncle was a brilliant, but hardhearted individual.

access   10. Some fallen branches bar the path to the gate.

——————— Unit 1 Review ———————

Choose a word from the Word List to complete the analogy.

Word List				
damage	convert	vibration	aorta	normal
eardrum	pulp	molars	publisher	ventricle
exhaustion	spasms	access	organs	crown

11. <u>Repair</u> is to _____ as <u>day</u> is to <u>night</u>.

12. <u>Summit</u> is to <u>mountain</u> as _____ is to <u>tree</u>.

13. <u>Stay</u> is to <u>maintain</u> as <u>change</u> is to _____ .

14. <u>Workout</u> is to _____ as <u>sleep</u> is to <u>relaxation</u>.

15. <u>Silence</u> is to <u>stillness</u> as <u>sound</u> is to _____ .

16. <u>Violin</u> is to <u>string</u> as <u>ear</u> is to _____ .

17. <u>Body</u> is to _____ as <u>house</u> is to <u>furniture</u>.

18. <u>Builder</u> is to <u>houses</u> as _____ is to <u>books</u>.

19. <u>Hard</u> is to <u>rock</u> as <u>soft</u> is to _____ .

20. <u>Roads</u> are to <u>highway</u> as <u>blood vessels</u> are to _____ .

On Top of the World!

Read this information about a mountain range. Think about the meanings of the words in bold type.

Did you see the movie *The Englishman Who Went Up a Hill and Came Down a Mountain*? This may sound like a strange title, but it makes perfect sense once you know the story. In the movie, the **inhabitants** of a small town in Wales have always assumed that a local **landform** was a mountain. One day a scientist proves them wrong. The landform, he says, is less than 300 meters (1,000 feet) tall. This makes it a hill, not a mountain. Like many movies, this one has a happy ending. The inhabitants simply add more soil to the **summit**.

No one, of course, doubts that the peaks in the Himalaya **range** are mountains. The word Himalaya means "abode of snow" in the Indian language of Sanskrit. The snow-capped peaks soar many thousands of feet above sea level. Mount Everest, at 29,064 feet (8,848 meters), is the world's highest.

How were these mountains formed? Long ago, all the continents were once joined together in a single supercontinent. The huge **landmass** is known as Pangaea, which means "all lands" in Greek. Over millions of years, Pangaea broke into pieces that began to drift away from one another. Between 40 million and 60 million years ago, the Indian subcontinent gradually **collided** with the rest of Asia. The land buckled and folded and piled up on top of itself. A mountain range took shape.

Between half a million and two million years ago, pressure from the collision reached a peak. The land folded and buckled further. As a result, the mountains soared another 10,000 feet (900 meters), making them not only the highest mountains in the world, but also the youngest. Amazingly, **geologists** say that the Himalayas are still growing, at a rate of about six inches a year. Someday, another peak may even surpass Everest!

Edit   **Create**   **Identify**

Classify
Label
Estimate

The View from the Top

Label the drawing with the correct vocabulary words.

" _____ think that the Indian subcontinent _____ with the Asian mainland. The collision caused the land to fold and buckle."

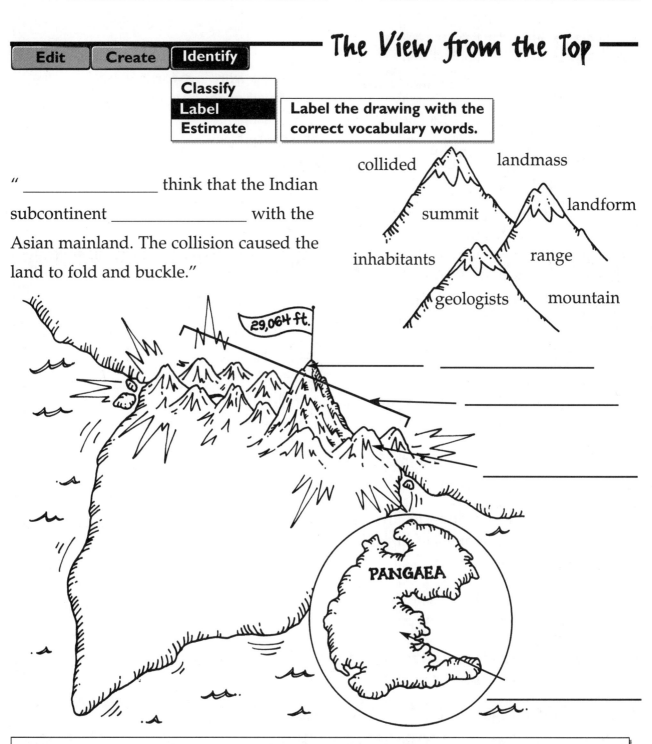

collided   landmass

summit   landform

inhabitants   range

geologists   mountain

29,064 ft.

PANGAEA

Also...

1. Hills and mountains are *landforms*. Find the names of the other two landforms.
2. Find out about the *inhabitants* of the Himalayas.

Research | Apply | **Process**

Replace
Classify
Define

Replace the word or words in bold type with a vocabulary word.

29,064 ft.

landmass   mountain   summit   collided
inhabitants

range   landform   geologists

Snowy Abode

1. On May 29, 1953, Edmund Hillary and Tenzing Norgay climbed to the **highest point**.   _____

2. Norgay, a Sherpa guide, was one of the **people that lives in a place** of the Himalaya region.   _____

3. The entire **group of mountains** spread out before them.   _____

4. The pair were the first to climb the world's highest **mass of land that rises to a great height**.   _____

5. The **feature of Earth's surface** they climbed was Mount Everest.   _____

6. **People who study Earth** say that the Himalayas are still growing.   _____

Mountain Building

Make a graphic relief map of India and Asia from clay. Use the map to demonstrate how the Himalayas were formed. Be sure to use the words *collided* and *landmass* in your explanation.

Whew! It's Getting Warmer!

Read this information about global warming. Think about the meanings of the words in bold type.

Do you know how gardeners and farmers grow plants when the weather is cold? They put their plants in a **greenhouse**. A greenhouse is a building made of glass. The sun shines in through the glass and warms the air inside.

Our Earth stays warm in the same way. It is surrounded—not by glass—but by a blanket of **invisible** gases. A few of the gases in our **atmosphere** act just like a greenhouse. The sun shines in, and the blanket of gases traps the heat like a roof. Without these gases, heat from the sun would simply hit the ground and bounce back into space. Earth would be as cold and uninviting as Mars.

For the past several thousand years, the level of gases in the air stayed about the same. Then in the mid-1700s, people began using **fossil fuels**, like coal, oil, and natural gas. As the fossil fuels burn, they release **carbon dioxide** into the air. Carbon dioxide acts like the glass in a greenhouse. It lets in the sun's warmth, but doesn't let it out. Before the 1700s, plants and marine animals were able to **absorb** the carbon dioxide. Now, however, they can't keep up with the increased levels.

If the levels of carbon dioxide continue to climb, our Earth may get warmer. Why is this a problem? As temperatures rise, ice near the North and South Poles would melt. Sea levels would rise and flood coastal areas. Some islands might be completely covered by water. Certain plants and animals might not be able to **adapt** to the warmer temperatures and would die out.

What can we do to stop the global warming? The answer is obvious. We must cut down on the amount of carbon dioxide that is being released into the air. How can we do this? Stop burning fossil fuels! Instead, we must use the power of the sun and the wind. **Solar** and wind power are the fuels of the future.

Name _____   Date _____

| Edit | Create | **Identify** |

| Find |
| **Label** |
| Define |

Label the drawing with the correct vocabulary words.

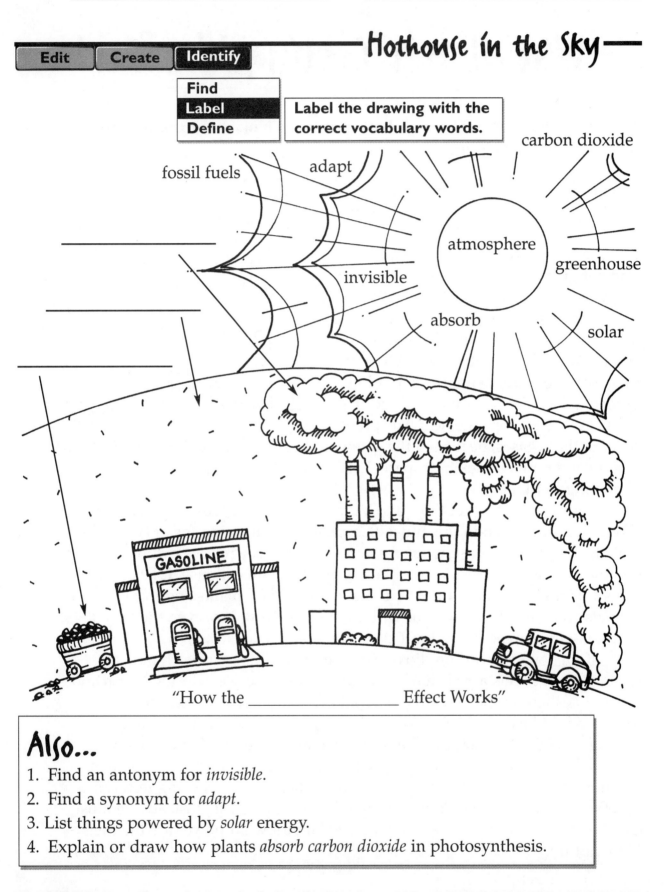

carbon dioxide

fossil fuels   adapt

atmosphere

greenhouse

invisible

absorb

solar

GASOLINE

"How the _____ Effect Works"

Also...

1. Find an antonym for *invisible*.
2. Find a synonym for *adapt*.
3. List things powered by *solar* energy.
4. Explain or draw how plants *absorb carbon dioxide* in photosynthesis.

Create Apply **Process**

Identify
Classify
Match

Classify the vocabulary words. Write the word that belongs in each group.

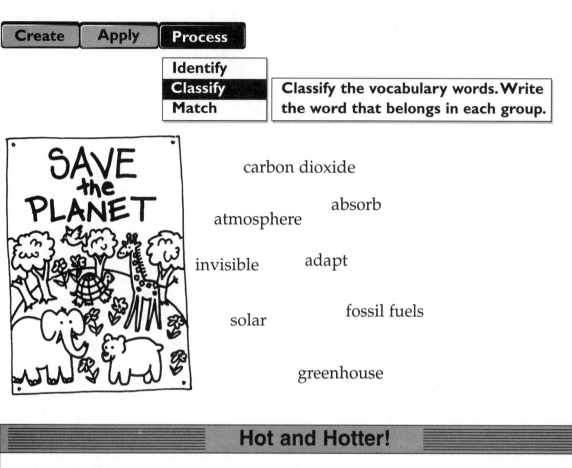

carbon dioxide

absorb

atmosphere

invisible   adapt

solar   fossil fuels

greenhouse

Hot and Hotter!

1. coal, oil, natural gas, _____
2. nitrogen, oxygen, _____
3. stratosphere, lithosphere, _____
4. summerhouse, hothouse, _____
5. stellar, lunar, _____
6. soak up, sponge, _____

Save the Planet!

Draw and label a poster urging people to decrease their dependence on fossil fuels. Use the words *invisible* and *adapt* in your explanation.

Killer Waves!

Read this story about a great explorer. Think about the meanings of the words in bold type.

If you were sailing on an ocean liner far out at sea, you might not notice it. Yet, it could be racing across the ocean at more than 300 miles an hour (500km/h). When it reaches the shore, it could reach a height of 100 feet (30 meters) and destroy everything in its path. What is it? *It* is a **tsunami** (tsoo-NAH-mee). That's the Japanese word for "great harbor wave." People sometimes call it a "tidal wave," but a tsunami has nothing to do with **tides**—the everyday rise and fall of the sea. Tides are caused by the pull of **gravity** between the moon and Earth. Nor are tsunamis caused by the wind—like ordinary waves.

What causes a tsunami? Usually the cause is an undersea **earthquake**. About four out of every five tsunamis take place within an area known as the "Ring of Fire." The area includes the coasts of North and South America and Japan, as well as islands in the western Pacific. Many volcanic **eruptions** and earthquakes occur in this zone. An earthquake lifts or drops part of the ocean floor. Then the water above it starts moving. This will start a tsunami's waves rolling across the ocean. The waves can travel thousands of miles outward from the earthquake's **epicenter**.

A tsunami works like a giant vacuum. Before it hits the shore, it sucks water from harbors and beaches. Fish flop helplessly on the bare sea floor. Boats are stranded. Then wave after wave blast ashore at 15-minute **intervals**. This can continue for two hours or more.

In the past century, tsunamis have killed more then 50,000 people. Recently, scientists have set up an early warning system to reduce the death toll. The Pacific Tsunami Warning System has a network of instruments to **detect** earthquakes that may cause these killer waves. Now, at least, scientists can warn people to move away from the shore before a killer wave strikes.

Edit   **Create**   **Identify**   ─── Start the Wave! ───

Label   Label the drawing with the
Find   correct vocabulary words.
Define

earthquake

intervals   detect   tsunami

tides

eruptions

epicenter   gravity

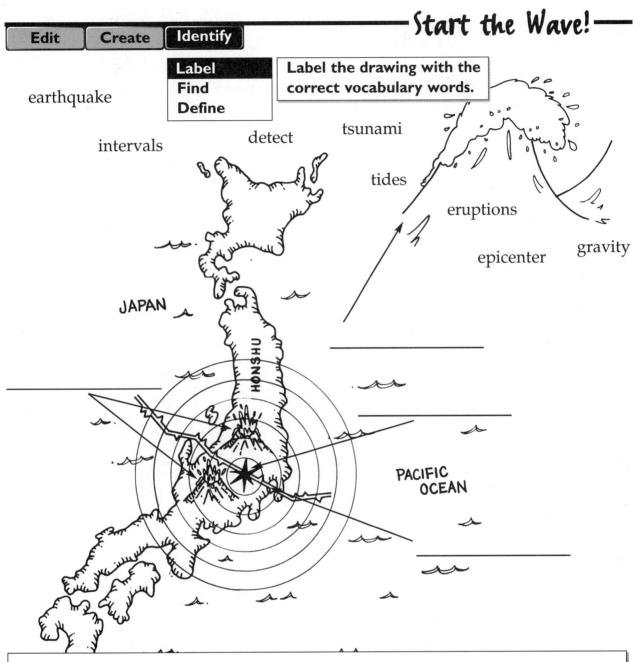

JAPAN

HONSHU

PACIFIC
OCEAN

Also...

1. Use a pencil to demonstrate the pull of *gravity*.
2. Solve this math problem. If tsunami waves come ashore at 15-minute *intervals*, how many waves will hit the shore in a two-hour period? in a three-hour period?
3. Use library resources to answer these questions:
   • What machine is used to *detect* earthquakes?
   • Are lakes affected by *tides*?

Create   Apply   **Process**

Classify
Find
Define

earthquake

Find the vocabulary word that fits each meaning.

detect   epicenter   tides   intervals

tsunami   eruptions   gravity

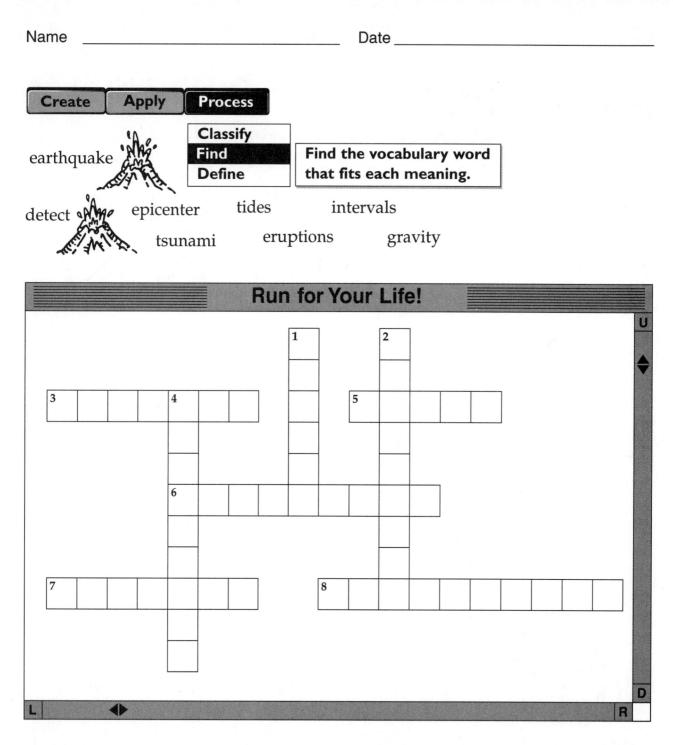

Run for Your Life!

ACROSS

3. the force that pulls things toward the center of Earth
5. the regular rise and fall of the water level of the oceans
6. the release of lava through volcanoes
7. a huge, powerful ocean wave
8. a trembling of the ground

DOWN

1. discover
2. the part of Earth's surface directly above the origin of an earthquake
4. periods of time between actions

——— Funnel Trouble! ———

Read this information about a tornado. Think about the meanings of the words in bold type.

In the movie *The Wizard of Oz*, Dorothy and her little dog Toto whirl through the air and land in the magical land of Oz. What brought them there? You know what it was. It was a **tornado**.

The word *tornado* probably comes from the Spanish word *tronada*, which means "thunderstorm." Tornadoes are also called cyclones or twisters. That's because a tornado has a **rotating**, spiraling column of air, called the **vortex**. Some tornadoes have a single vortex. Others have a funnel that has several vortexes within it. Vortexes vary from 15 to 500 yards in **diameter**.

The first sign of a tornado is often a whirlwind of dust swirling upward from the ground. At the same time, a short **funnel** grows from the storm cloud above it. The funnel **descends** further from the cloud and touches the ground. Some funnels speed along at 70 miles per hour. Others remain practically still, spinning over a single spot. Tornadoes leave a path of death and destruction. Their winds are the strongest and fastest on Earth.

What causes these storms? Scientists don't know for sure. What they do know is that **conditions** are best in the Mississippi River valley. Here, especially in the springtime, warm, **moist** air moves in from the Gulf of Mexico. As warm air rises from the ground, it meets the winds blowing in from the south. As the air continues to rise, it meets winds from the west and the southwest. The rising air begins to rotate. Clouds develop. The clouds grow larger and turn into thunderstorms. The rotation of the rising air will eventually become the rotation of the thunderstorm and some of the rotation of the tornado.

If you ever hear a weather forecaster predict a tornado, get below ground. You don't want to join Dorothy in Oz—even if it is a magical place.

Edit | Create | Identify | ——— Tornado Alley ———

Label
Classify
Order

Label the drawing with the correct vocabulary words.

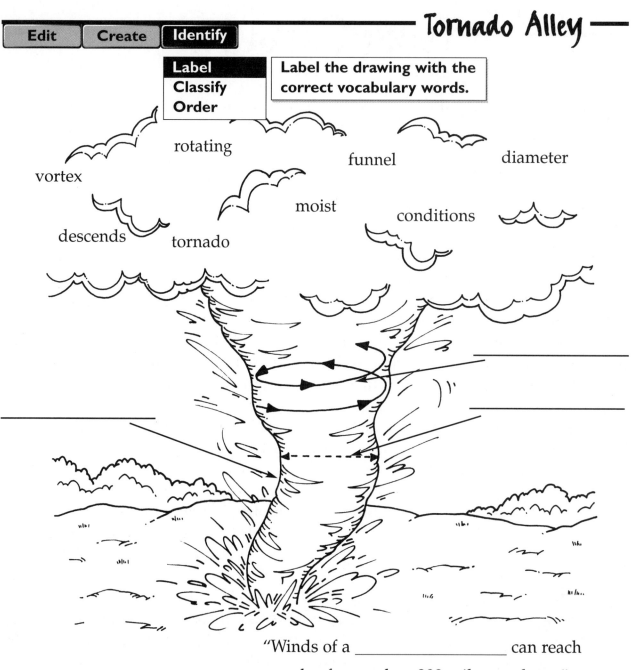

rotating

vortex

funnel   diameter

moist

descends   conditions

tornado

"Winds of a _____ can reach speeds of more than 300 miles per hour."

Also...

1. Explain the causes of a tornado. Use the words *conditions, moist,* and *descends* in your answer.

2. Draw the *funnel* of a tornado. Draw arrows to show the direction of the winds inside the *vortex*.

Create   **Research**   **Process**

moist

Find
Add
Complete

Complete each pair of sentences
with the correct vocabulary word.

rotating   diameter

funnel

descends

vortex

conditions

tornado

Whirling Fury

1. A balloon ascends into the air.
   A submarine _____ into the ocean.

2. The circumference is the distance around a circle.
   The _____ is the distance through the center of the circle.

3. The air in a desert is dry.
   The air in a rain forest is _____ .

4. A box has the shape of a cube.
   A _____ has the shape of a cone.

5. The moon is orbiting the earth.
   The earth is _____ on its axis.

6. A hurricane can last several days or weeks.
   A _____ can last several seconds or minutes.

Violent Weather

1. Compare the sizes of a small and large *vortex*. Put two stakes 15 yards apart on the playground. Put two stakes 100 yards apart.

2. Make a chart listing the *conditions* that cause thunderstorms, hurricanes, and blizzards.

Coral Reefs

Read this information about coral reefs. Think about the meanings of the words in bold type.

Along the northeast coast of Australia lies the Great Barrier Reef. It stretches in an unbroken chain for 2,000 kilometers (1,250 miles), making it the world's largest reef formation. The reef is a great tourist attraction. Visitors look at the pink, yellow, blue, purple, and green **coral** through glass-bottom boats. Swimmers and divers get a first-hand view of the amazing variety of creatures that inhabit the reef. There are giant clams so big that you could use their shells as bathtubs. At night, ghost crabs scuttle upon the reef's beaches in search of insects and other small animals.

The Great Barrier Reef is just what its name suggests—a **barrier reef**. This kind of reef lies offshore, separated from the land by a **lagoon**, water that is more than 10 meters (about 30 feet) deep. There are two other reef forms—**atolls** and **fringing reefs**. Fringing reefs are located close to shore. Only shallow water separates them from land. Atolls, on the other hand, are found far offshore. These ring-shaped reefs usually enclose a circular lagoon.

All reefs, no matter what kind, are formed in the same way. They are built by countless numbers of tiny coral **polyps**. A polyp is an animal that is no larger than your fingernail and is often only the size of a pinhead. Its body is shaped like a tube with **tentacles** at one end. The polyps build hard, cup-shaped skeletons around their soft bodies. These protect them from their enemies, and at the same time form part of the coral reef.

Corals usually live together in **colonies**. Side by side, the polyps build their skeletons. As the animals die, more polyps build skeletons on top of theirs. Coral reefs grow slowly, usually at the rate of only a few centimeters each year. It took polyps more than two million years to build the Great Barrier Reef. It is the largest structure ever created by any animal.

South Sea Paradise

| Edit | Create | **Identify** |

| **Label** |
| Classify |
| Order |

Label the drawing with the correct vocabulary words.

lagoon   coral

tentacles   atolls

fringing reefs   polyps

colonies

barrier reef

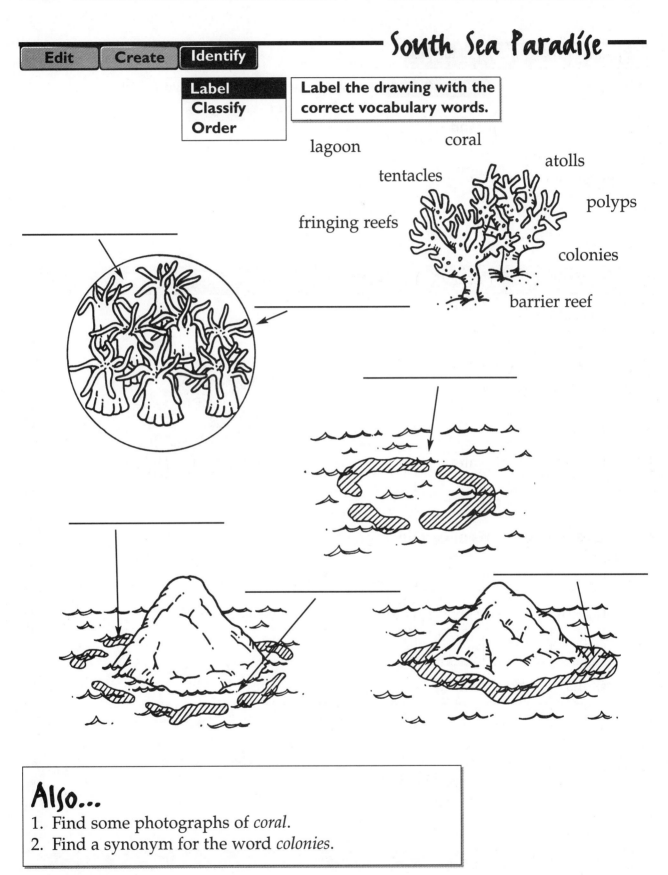

_____

_____

_____   _____

Also...

1. Find some photographs of *coral*.
2. Find a synonym for the word *colonies*.

Create   **Apply**   **Process**

Identify
Match
Find

Identify the vocabulary word that fits each meaning.

polyps

lagoon   fringing reefs   coral   atolls

barrier reef   tentacles   colonies

Take a Dive

coral animals

			8		1

the skeletons of tiny sea animals

			7	

a shallow body of water

				4

long, thin body parts of certain animals

2							

groups of animals of the same kind that live together

			3		

reefs that are close to land

		5				6			

Write the numbered letters in the puzzle. You will discover the name of an animal that lives on the reef.

1	2	3	4	5		6	7	8

Unit 11 Review

Replace the word or words in bold type with a vocabulary word. Circle the vocabulary word. Read the sentence again to check your answer.

1. A sponge can **soak up** a lot of water.

   adapt   absorb   detect

2. A short **period of time between two events** passed before he answered my letter.

   interval   range   diameter

3. The climbers reached the **highest point** just before noon.

   atmosphere   landmass   summit

4. The airplane **moved from a higher to a lower place** for a landing.

   descended   rotated   collided

5. We swam in the **shallow body of water**.

   coral   tide   lagoon

6. I **notice** the presence of anger in your voice.

   funnel   detect   descend

7. Were the **residents** of the island friendly?

   inhabitants   geologists   polyps

8. **A violent, whirling wind** can be very destructive.

   A volcano   An earthquake   A tornado

9. **Coral islands** are common in the Pacific Ocean.

   Atolls   Colonies   Epicenters

10. Air is **not able to be seen**.

    moist   invisible   rotating

Unit II Review

Complete the analogies with the correct word from the Word List.

Word List

colonies	invisible	eruptions	geologists	vortex
polyps	collided	solar	funnel	greenhouse
atmosphere	moist	tides	tentacles	gravity

11. _____ are to <u>rocks</u> as <u>astronomers</u> are to <u>space</u>.

12. <u>Floating</u> is to <u>weightlessness</u> as <u>pull</u> is to _____ .

13. <u>Soaked</u> is to _____ as <u>parched</u> is to <u>dry</u>.

14. <u>Apex</u> is to <u>top</u> as _____ is to <u>center</u>.

15. <u>Elk</u> are to <u>herds</u> as <u>ants</u> are to _____ .

16. <u>Octopi</u> are to _____ as <u>spiders</u> are to <u>legs</u>.

17. <u>Earthquakes</u> are to <u>tremors</u> as <u>volcanoes</u> are to _____ .

18. <u>Fossil fuel</u> is to <u>coal</u> as _____ is to the <u>sun</u>.

19. <u>Ice</u> is to <u>freezer</u> as <u>plants</u> are to _____ .

20. <u>Passed</u> is to <u>missed</u> as <u>hit</u> is to _____ .

—————Is There Life on Mars?—————

Read this information about the possibility of life on Mars. Think about the meanings of the words in bold type.

About 600,000 years ago, **meteorites** from the planet Mars landed on Antarctica. There the chunks of rock lay until August of 1996, when American scientists found them. They took pictures of the rocks with microscopes. The pictures show that they contain the fossil remains of ancient Martian **microbes**. The discovery of the tiny **organisms** caused a great deal of excitement in the scientific world. They raised the possibility that life still exists on Mars.

　　To try to solve the mystery, space **missions** are flying to Mars. The first, the *Mars Pathfinder*, landed on Mars on July 4, 1997. The next day, a small **robotic** vehicle left the spacecraft. The *Sojourner*, which was about the size of a small suitcase, explored the surface of Mars. It traveled several hundred feet from the spacecraft, testing rocks with its specially designed **probe**. Another mission, the *Mars Global Surveyor*, began to **orbit** Mars in September 1997.

　　These early **missions** searched for life, past or present, and for evidence of liquid water or ice. Without water, life cannot exist. Long ago, Mars may have had huge oceans and a dense atmosphere. But, sometime in the last three billion years, the climate changed dramatically. Mars would have lost most of its air and all of its surface water. The water would not disappear, though. It would still exist somewhere, in polar ice caps or in underground lakes.

　　In 2001, the *Odyssey* probe reached Mars, sending back information that finally confirmed the existence of abundant water on the planet. NASA scientists have selected two sites for future landings on Mars in 2003. Perhaps these missions will find evidence of life in outer space. Or perhaps the mystery will continue.

43

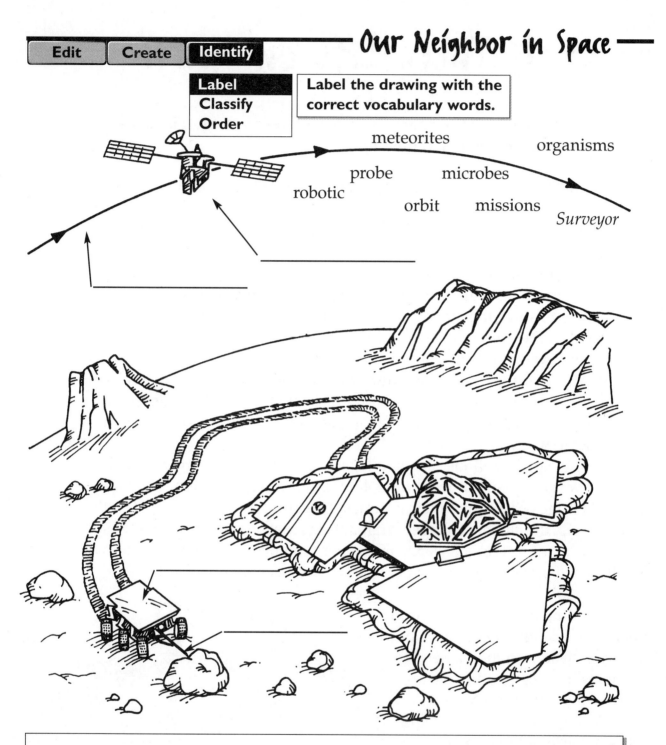

Edit **Create** **Identify** ― **Our Neighbor in Space** ―

| **Label** |
| **Classify** |
| **Order** |

Label the drawing with the correct vocabulary words.

meteorites   organisms

probe   microbes

robotic

orbit   missions

Surveyor

Also...

Write two headlines for newspaper articles about discovering the fossil remains of ancient Martian microbes on Antarctica. Use the words *microbes*, *organisms*, and *meteorites* in your headlines. Write a headline for new *missions*.

Create   **Apply**   **Process**

Identify
Classify
Match

Classify the vocabulary words. Write
the word that belongs in each group.

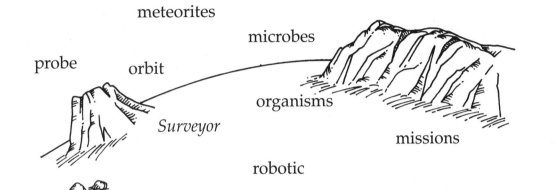

meteorites

microbes

probe   orbit

organisms

Surveyor

missions

robotic

Mission to Mars

1. *Viking*, *Pathfinder*, _____

2. asteroids, meteors, _____

3. maneuvers, actions, _____

4. bacteria, germs, _____ or _____

5. path, route, _____

6. antenna, arm, _____

Exploring Mars

1. Draw a picture of a *robotic* vehicle.

2. Write a caption for your picture.

Balloons on Parade!

Read this story about some giant air sculptures. Think about the meanings of the words in bold type.

Every Thanksgiving Day for the past 70 years, people from all over the world have flocked to New York City to see a parade of giant air **sculptures**. In past years, the parade has included the Pink Panther, Spiderman, Bart Simpson, Peter Rabbit, Betty Boop, Woody Woodpecker, Bullwinkle, and Beethoven the dog. The six-story-high superheroes—about 18 characters in all—twist and dance over the heads of **spectators** lining the parade route. Beneath each balloon is a crew of 40 volunteers who hang tightly onto guide ropes.

How are these giant air sculptures made? First a **designer** draws sketches of the character. When everyone at the studio is satisfied with the design, the designer makes a fiberglass model and paints it to look like the finished balloon. The actual balloon is made of nylon and consists of several different sections, or **chambers**. For example, Spiderman's head, hands, arms, chest, and feet are each separate chambers. This way, if one chamber punctures, the entire balloon won't **deflate**. Workers seal the seams with heat, and artists paint the balloon. It takes six months to complete the process.

On Wednesday evening, the deflated balloons are shipped from New Jersey to New York's Upper West Side. Workers spread out the balloons on the street. They **tether** the balloons with nets and anchor them with sandbags so they don't take off. Then they slowly fill them with air and a gas called **helium**. They fill one chamber at a time, from top to bottom. The job of **inflating** the balloons lasts until well past midnight.

You can watch the parade on television. But you have to be there to get the best view. If you go, bring your camera and lots of film. Also, bring a milk crate— unless you're seven feet tall. One year the crowd was 13 people deep. If you stand on a crate, you'll be able to see the floats and marching bands.

Blown Up Words

Edit **Create** **Identify**

Label
Find
Match

Label the drawing with the correct vocabulary words.

spectators
inflating
sculptures
tether
helium
deflate
chambers
designer

Also...

1. Demonstrate how workers *deflate* a balloon.
2. Demonstrate how workers *tether* a balloon.
3. List the materials a *designer* uses.

Workers are _____

one of several of the balloon's

_____ .

Research   **Apply**   **Process**

Replace   **Replace the word or words in bold**
Classify   **type with a vocabulary word.**
Define

helium

designer
tether   inflating

spectators   chambers

deflate   sculptures   tether

Rise to the Occasion

1. The giant air **figures** floated above our heads.   _____

2. Thousands of **observers** lined both sides of the street.   _____

3. The night before the parade, we watched the workers fill the balloons with **a gas that is lighter than air**.   _____

4. Each balloon has many **enclosed spaces**.   _____

5. The job of **putting air into** the balloons took hours.   _____

6. Workers had to **bind** the balloons with rope to keep them from floating away.   _____

7. After the parade, we watched the workers **release the gas from** the balloons.   _____

8. Maybe we will get a chance to meet the **person who made the patterns**.   _____

Be a Balloonatic!

Imagine you are a designer of giant air sculptures. Draw a picture of your favorite character. Draw lines to separate the chambers. Write a caption for your picture.

— Photography's Early Beginnings —

Read this information about the development of the camera. Think about the meanings of the words in bold type.

Isaac Newton once said, "If I have seen further (than other men), it is by standing upon the shoulders of giants." Newton knew that an invention is often the work of several people. The camera is a perfect example of this.

For centuries scientists and artists had used a device called the camera obscura, which means "the dark chamber." It was a darkened room with a tiny hole in one wall. Light coming through the opening formed an **image** on the opposite wall. The image was an **inverted**—upside-down—picture of the scene outside. Scientists used the camera obscura to view eclipses of the sun. Artists used it as a sketching aid. They traced the lines and shapes of the image.

The first camera obscura was large enough for a man to enter. By the early 1600s, artists began using a tent instead of a room. They carried the tent into the countryside to sketch landscapes. Later, the image-making device became even more **portable**. By the 1660s, it was a box about two feet long with a **lens** placed over the hole. The lens made the image larger and sharper.

The camera obscura was the first camera. It provided a way to **project** an image onto a piece of paper. But scientists wanted to find a way to make the image permanent. The first person to do this was Joseph Niépce. He **exposed** a metal plate in the camera for as long as 30 minutes. Then he **engraved**, or carved, the image on the plate to "fix" it. His were the first **photographs**. In 1839 his partner, Louis J. M. Daguerre, improved the process. He developed the image with mercury vapor and "fixed" it with common salt.

From then on, improvements came rapidly. Exposure times shortened, the size of the image grew, and the size of the camera shrank. Before long, everyone could be a photographer.

Edit   **Create**   **Identify**   ── Seizing the Light ──

Label
Order
Find

Label the drawing with the correct vocabulary words.

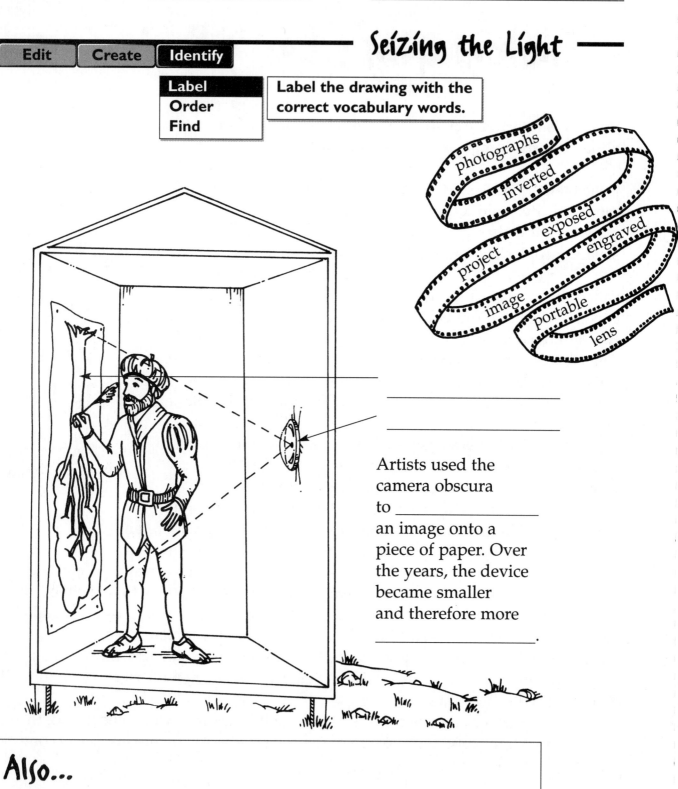

photographs
inverted
exposed
engraved
project
image
portable
lens

Artists used the camera obscura to _____ an image onto a piece of paper. Over the years, the device became smaller and therefore more

_____

Also...

1. Find a synonym for *exposed*.
2. Demonstrate how an artist *engraved* a design on a metal plate.
3. Use *photographs* to demonstrate the meaning of *inverted*.

Name_____ Date _____

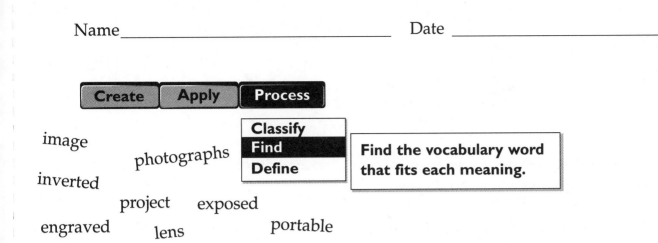

Create | Apply | Process

Classify
Find
Define

image

photographs

inverted

project   exposed

engraved   lens   portable

Find the vocabulary word that fits each meaning.

Say "Cheese!"

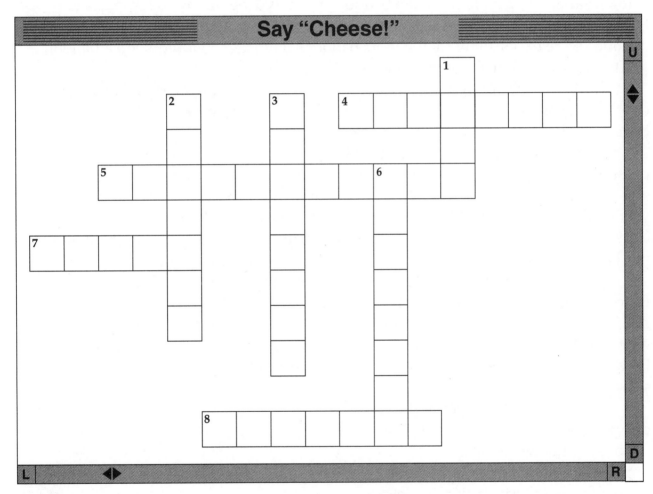

ACROSS
4. upside-down
5. pictures formed on film by a camera
7. a picture of a person or thing
8. allowed light to reach a photographic film or plate

DOWN
1. a clear, curved piece of glass
2. cause an image to appear on a surface
3. carved a figure or design into stone, metal, or wood
6. easy to carry from place to place

Ships of the Air

Read this information about a special kind of aircraft. Think about the meanings of the words in bold type.

People have always dreamed of flying, but it was not until 1783 that the dream finally came true. That's when two Frenchmen took to the air in a hot-air balloon. A few years later, people filled the balloons with **hydrogen**. Though the gas is highly **flammable**—it burns easily—inventors realized that hydrogen-filled balloons were easier to fly than hot-air balloons. Hydrogen would keep a balloon **aloft** longer, and it could lift more weight.

Both hot-air and hydrogen balloons had problems, however. A balloon can only go where the wind takes it. To be useful as **transportation**, a balloon would have to have a power source and be able to be steered.

In 1852 a French engineer, Henri Giffard, hung a **gondola**—the car in which passengers ride—beneath a cigar-shaped hydrogen balloon. The gondola had a steam engine and a **propeller**. This was the first true **dirigible**. In the next few years, inventors developed bigger dirigibles and lighter and more powerful engines. Though a dirigible moved along at a top speed of only about 85 miles per hour, it could carry heavy loads and large numbers of passengers.

Soon the giant airships began making regular passenger flights in Europe and between Europe and South America or the United States. They were magnificent machines. Some were more than 700 feet (210 meters) long. The gondolas had lounges, cabins, dining rooms, and decks with picture windows. Passengers, who were free to move around, watched Earth slowly pass below them.

Unfortunately, the era of the great dirigibles was short-lived. In 1937, as the airship the *Hindenburg* approached the **mooring mast** at the Lakehurst Naval Air Station in New Jersey, it exploded, killing 35 of the 97 passengers. No more airships were ever built.

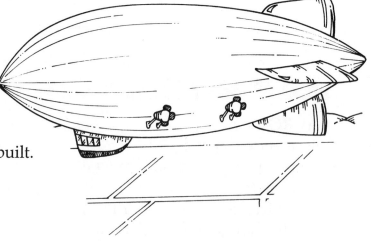

Name_____ Date _____

| Edit | Create | Identify |

Label
Order
Find

Label the drawing with the correct vocabulary words.

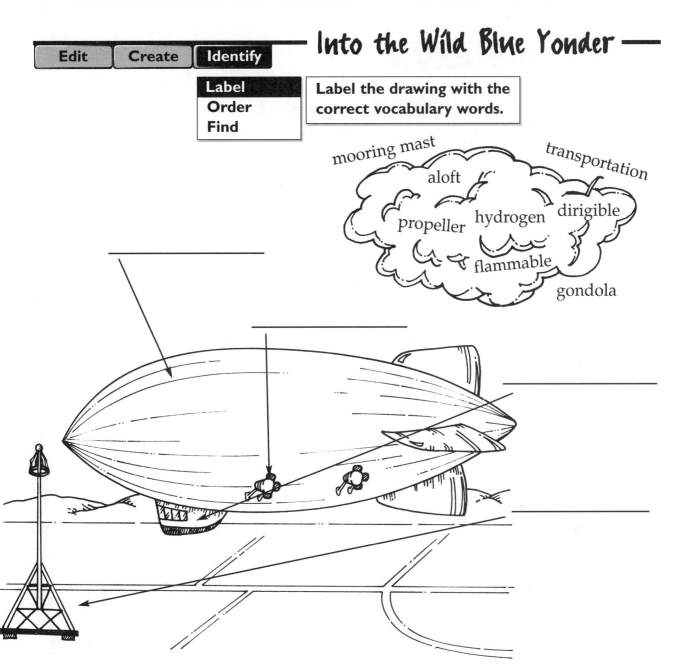

mooring mast   transportation

aloft

propeller   hydrogen   dirigible

flammable

gondola

Also...

1. Explain why *dirigibles* were dangerous. Use the words *hydrogen* and *flammable* in your answer.
2. Write an ad for a *dirigible*. Use the word *transportation* in your ad.
3. Find a synonym for *aloft*.

Create **Research** **Process**

Find
Complete
Add

Complete each pair of sentences with the correct vocabulary word.

dirigible

flammable

propeller

transportation

aloft

mooring mast

hydrogen

gondola

Lighter-Than-Air Travel

1. Water is a liquid.
   _____ is a gas.
2. A boat has a sail.
   A helicopter has a _____ .
3. Passengers on a airplane sit in the cabin.
   Passengers on an airship stay in the _____ .
4. An airplane is heavier than air.
   A _____ is lighter than air.
5. A submarine can stay submerged.
   A hot-air balloon can stay _____ .
6. Helium is safe; it will not burn.
   Hydrogen is dangerous; it is _____ .

U

D

L ◄► R

Up, Up, and Away!

Design an airship or spacecraft for the future.

U

D

L ◄► R

Name_____ Date _____

Her Royal Deepness

Read this information about an underwater explorer. Think about the meanings of the words in bold type.

With a thump the **aquanaut** landed on the floor of the Pacific Ocean, 1,250 feet (381 meters) below the surface. September 19, 1979, was a **memorable** date for the underwater explorer and for the scientific world. It was the first time a person had walked so deeply underwater, yet was unconnected to surface support.

Sylvia Earle had begun her voyage strapped to a **platform** on the front of a small **submersible** named *Star II*. When the submersible reached the ocean floor, she freed herself from the platform and took a few small steps. Sylvia was wearing a diving suit nicknamed Jim. Like the suits worn by astronauts, the Jim supplied her with air, **maintained** a comfortable temperature, and protected her from outside conditions. At these depths the water pressure is so great that no one could survive without **protective** gear. On land we experience about 14.7 pounds (6.7 kilograms) of atmospheric pressure all over our bodies. Where Sylvia stood, the pressure is about 600 pounds (272.2 kilograms)! That's enough pressure to cause the air spaces in the lungs, ears, and sinuses to burst.

Sylvia, a marine biologist, has been diving most of her life. Diving enables her to study underwater plants and animals in their own habitat. After her historic dive, she wanted to go even deeper. With the help of engineer Graham Hawkes, Sylvia designed a new submersible. *Deep Rover* is lightweight, battery-operated, and simple to use. Instead of having small portholes, the vehicle is **transparent** and provides excellent all-around views. It also has a suction device, or "slurp gun," for collecting **aquatic** plants and animals.

On *Deep Rover*, Sylvia broke her own record for deep solo diving. In 1983 she descended 3,000 feet (900 meters) off the coast of California. Now, she is working on a new submersible, *Deep Flight*. Who knows where it will take "Her Royal Deepness"?

Beneath the Waves

Edit   Create   Identify

Label
Order
Find

Label the drawing with the correct vocabulary words.

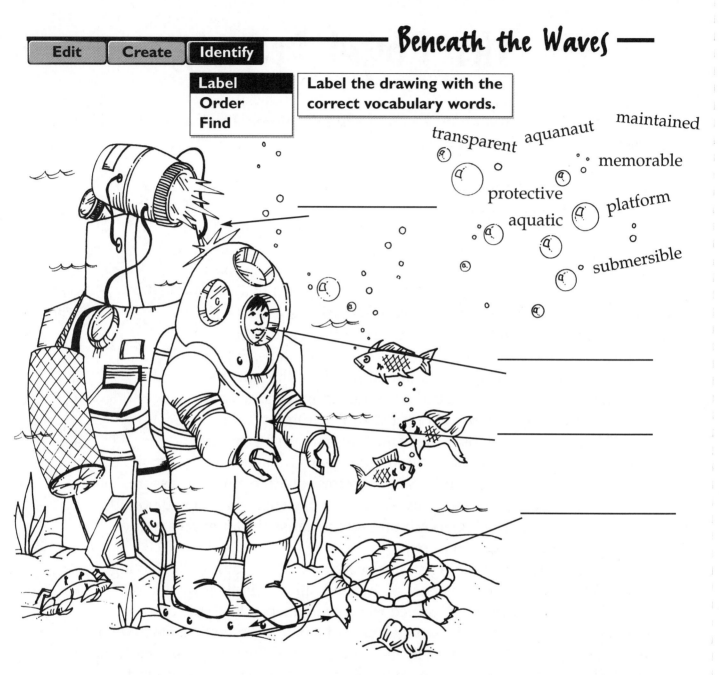

transparent   aquanaut   maintained

memorable

protective

aquatic   platform

submersible

_____

_____

_____

_____

The diver wore _____ gear that _____ a comfortable temperature and supplied her with air.

Also...

1. Explain why Sylvia Earle's dive was a *memorable* event.
2. Find an antonym for *transparent*.
3. Name some *aquatic* plants and animals.

Name_____ Date _____

| Research | Apply | Process |

Identify
Match
Find

Identify the vocabulary word that fits each meaning.

transparent   aquanaut   maintained

protective

platform

aquatic

submersible   memorable

Onward and Downward

any underwater craft

		1								

living in or growing in water

	2						5	

allowing light to pass through so that things on the other side can be clearly seen

	6										

worth remembering

	3							

a raised, flat surface

	7				4			

Write the numbered letters in the puzzle. You will discover the name of a tiny sea animal that can illuminate itself.

1	2	3	1	4	4		5	4	6	2	7

— Unit III Review —

The sentences on this page show how words that are alike can be compared. Read the sentences, and think about the meanings of the underlined words. Write the word that completes each sentence in the blank.

1. <u>Astronaut</u> is to <u>space</u> as _____ is to <u>ocean</u>.

       gondola   **aquanaut**   **mission**

2. <u>Camera</u> is to_____ as <u>television</u> is to <u>screen</u>.

       lens   **chamber**   **platform**

3. <u>Liquid</u> is to <u>water</u> as gas is to_____.

       flammable   **helium**   **gondola**

4. <u>Glass</u> is to _____ as <u>fog</u> is to <u>cloudy</u>.

       protective   **inverted**   **transparent**

5. <u>Britannia</u> is to <u>yacht</u> as <u>Hindenburg</u> is to _____.

       dirigible   **probe**   **transportation**

6. <u>Track</u> is to <u>train</u> as _____ is to <u>planet</u>.

       aquatic   **orbit**   **platform**

7. <u>Building</u> is to <u>stationary</u> as <u>tent</u> is to _____.

       portable   **flammable**   **submersible**

8. <u>Perform</u> is to <u>actors</u> as <u>observe</u> is to _____.

       sculptures   **photographs**   **spectators**

9. <u>Airplane</u> is to _____ as <u>ship</u> is to <u>afloat</u>.

       exposed   **aloft**   **tether**

10. <u>Huge</u> is to <u>elephants</u> as <u>tiny</u> is to _____.

        microbes   **missions**   **sculptures**

———— Unit III Review ————

Choose the word from the Word List that is most similar to the clues.

Word List

					U
probe	submersible	flammable	chambers	tether	
gondola	hydrogen	aquatic	memorable	inverted	
deflate	image	missions	platform	designer	

L ◄► R D

11. oxygen, nitrogen, _____

12. errand, calling, _____

13. reflect, portray, _____

14. explode, puncture, _____

15. marine, oceanic, _____

16. capsized, overturned, _____

17. rooms, berths, _____

18. great, unforgettable, _____

19. instrument, tool, _____

20. basket, car, _____

— New Zealand's Giant Insects —

Read this information about an unusual insect. Think about the meanings of the words in bold type.

China is famous for its giant **pandas**. Australia is home to the kangaroo as well as other **marsupials**. New Zealand, too, has an animal found nowhere else on Earth. This animal, however, is one with which you may not be familiar.

Here, on this island nation located in the vast reaches of the South Pacific, lives an insect about the size of a house mouse. New Zealanders call their wingless, cricket-like insects **wetas**. Because few mammal **predators** lived on the islands of New Zealand, birds and insects often **evolved** into awkward, flightless creatures. The giant weta is no exception. The insects have changed little in 200 million years and are among the country's oldest native life forms.

There are about ten different **species** of giant wetas. The largest, which weigh in at 2.5 ounces (170 grams), beat most of the world's insects in weight and bulk. Most wetas live in lowland forests, but the mountain weta thrives beneath rocks above the tree line. Tree wetas are found throughout the country.

Although some of their **habitats** have been destroyed, most species have adjusted to changes brought by humans. However, they do have to deal with predators, like rats, that are not native to New Zealand but were brought in from other places. While the giant wetas can scare away smaller predators by lashing out with their spiny back legs, they're defenseless against a predator the size of a rat.

Wetas may not be as appealing as giant pandas, but they are unique. As a result, the government has stepped up its efforts to protect wetas and other **endangered** species. After all, where but in New Zealand can you feed a carrot to a handful of legs and spines!

The Land Down Under

Edit   **Create**   **Identify**

Label
Classify
Order

Label the drawing with the correct vocabulary words.

marsupials   pandas
wetas
predators   evolved
species   habitats

endangered

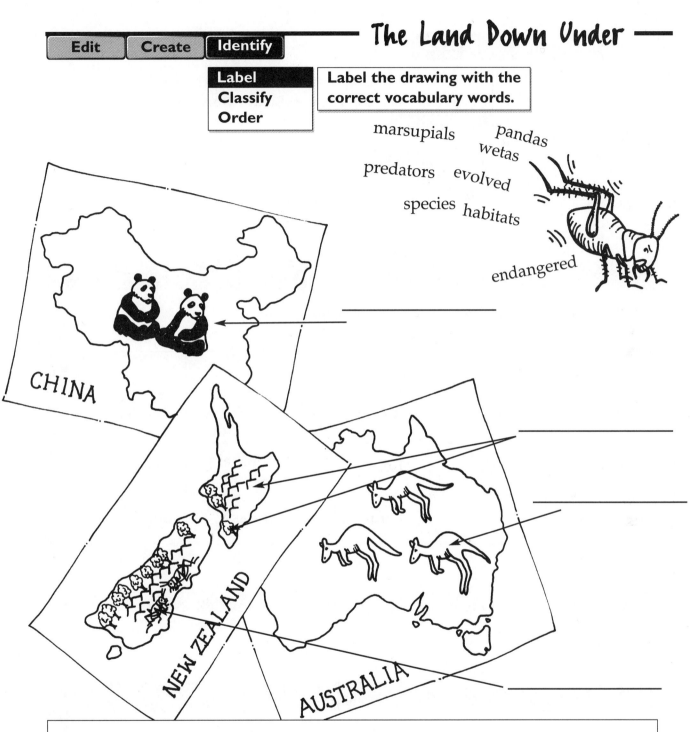

CHINA

NEW ZEALAND

AUSTRALIA

_____

_____

_____

_____

Also...

1. List or draw some *endangered species*.

2. List some *predators*.

3. Find a synonym for *evolved*.

Name_____ Date _____

Research   Apply   **Process**

Classify
Graphs
Charts

Complete the chart with the
correct vocabulary words.

marsupials

wetas

predators

pandas

endangered

species

habitats

evolved

A Bug-Lover's Dream

Complete the chart with the correct vocabulary words.

	Insects			
kangaroos	crickets	tigers	American alligator	grassland
possums	beetles	lions	mountain zebra	forest
bandicoots		leopards	pandas	desert

Australia's Amazing Animals

Find facts about the marsupials of Australia. Use
the words *evolved* and *species* in your report.

Name_____ Date _____

— The World's Largest Flower —

Read this information about an unusual flower. Think about the meanings of the words in bold type.

You probably can identify many of nature's champions. The blue whale holds the record as the largest mammal, while the giant sequoia is the largest tree. What you may not know is the name of the world's largest flower. That title belongs to a little-known **specimen** called *Rafflesia arnoldii*.

Rafflesia arnoldii was discovered by Sir Thomas Raffles, the British founder of Singapore. In 1818 he and a **naturalist** named Joseph Arnold were exploring the **rain forest** of Sumatra. They stumbled across a gigantic flower measuring more than a yard across its petals and weighing 15 pounds! It was named *Rafflesia arnoldii* in their honor.

Rafflesia arnoldii is not only the largest flower in the world but also one of the rarest. It blooms only on the islands of Sumatra and Borneo. It is a jungle **parasite**, which means that it has no roots, no stems, and no leaves. Instead, it grows from tiny seeds on the roots or lower stems of wild grape vines. **Filaments** spread out from the seeds inside the vine. About a year and a half will pass before a bud bulges through the surface. The buds, which look like large heads of cabbage, grow for nine months before flowering.

Size is not the only amazing thing about this flower. Its orange petal-like **lobes** feel leathery to the touch. They are covered with pale patches, some of which are raised like warts. The flower gives off a smell that is similar to rotting meat. The odor draws flies that **pollinate** it.

Very few people have ever seen a *Rafflesia arnoldii*. That's because it grows deep in the rain forest. Moreover, the flower blossoms and wilts within four days. Within a few weeks, *Rafflesia arnoldii* **dissolves** into a slimy mass.

Name_____ Date _____

| Edit | Create | Identify |

| Label |
| Classify |
| Order |

Label the drawing with the correct vocabulary words.

specimen   naturalist

rain forest

parasite   filaments

lobes

pollinate

dissolves

_____

_____

_____

_____

_____

Also...

1. Demonstrate how a powder *dissolves* in water.

2. Find the names of other plants that are *parasites*.

3. Explain how bees *pollinate* a flower.

Name_____ Date _____

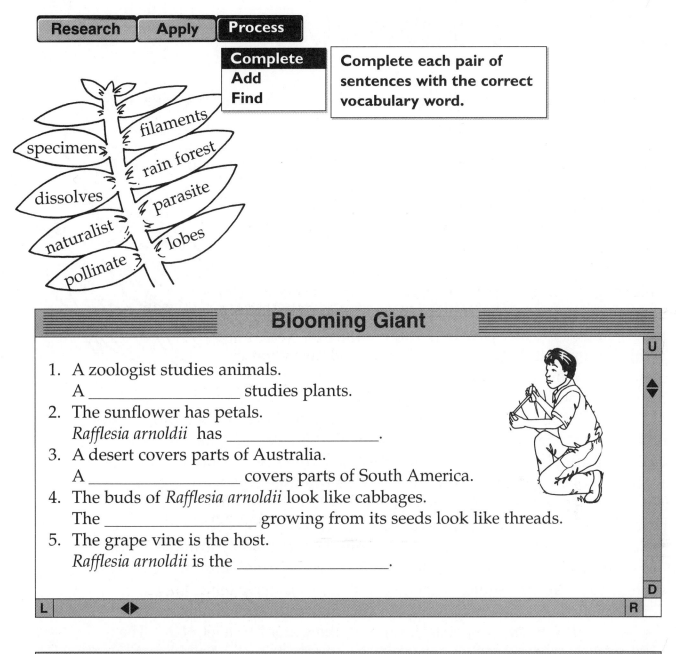

Research   Apply   Process

Complete
Add
Find

Complete each pair of
sentences with the correct
vocabulary word.

filaments
specimen
rain forest
dissolves
parasite
naturalist
lobes
pollinate

Blooming Giant

1. A zoologist studies animals.
   A _____ studies plants.
2. The sunflower has petals.
   Rafflesia arnoldii has _____.
3. A desert covers parts of Australia.
   A _____ covers parts of South America.
4. The buds of *Rafflesia arnoldii* look like cabbages.
   The _____ growing from its seeds look like threads.
5. The grape vine is the host.
   Rafflesia arnoldii is the _____.

Eureka! I found it!

Imagine you have just discovered a new plant. Write a journal entry telling
about your discovery. Use the words *specimen*, *pollinate*, and *dissolves* in
your entry. Draw a picture of the plant.

Ocean Giant

Read this information about a giant octopus. Think about the meanings of the words in bold type.

Long ago, sailors thought that the oceans were full of all kinds of terrible sea monsters. They told tales of a giant **octopus** that destroyed ships and plucked men from the decks like pieces of candy. Amazingly, there is some truth to the tale. While the giant octopus is not the monster the sailors imagined, it is huge. The average adult male weighs about 50 pounds (23 kilograms). The arms span an average of eight feet (25 meters). However, no one knows for sure how big these animals get. One octopus found off the western coast of Canada weighed about 600 pounds (272 kilograms). Its arm span was over 31 feet (9.6 meters).

Despite its size, the giant octopus is a shy creature. It often prowls the ocean floor at night looking for food. Though it is shy, the octopus is also very curious. **Biologists** think it is the smartest of all the **invertebrates**—animals without backbones. It probably has the same **intelligence** as a house cat.

Like all octopuses, the Pacific giant belongs to a group of **mollusks**—animals with hard outer shells—called cephalopods. The word cephalopod means "headfooted." The name comes from the fact that the arms seem to grow directly out of its head. Octopuses have eight arms. Most of the other cephalopods, like the squid, cuttlefish, and nautilus, have ten or more.

The octopus moves by using the **suckers** on its arms to crawl over the bottom. It can also propel itself through the water like a jet plane. The octopus does this by sucking water into its **mantle**, the baglike area in back of its eyes. Then it forces out the water through a **siphon**. To escape from enemies, the octopus squirts a blackish ink. Once biologists thought the ink was just a smoke screen. Now they think the cloud takes on the shape of an octopus. While the predator tries to decide what to attack, the real octopus makes a getaway.

Citizen of the Sea

| Edit | Create | Identify |

Label
Classify
Order

Label the drawing with the correct vocabulary words.

octopus

siphon   suckers

biologists

invertebrates   mantle

intelligence

mollusks

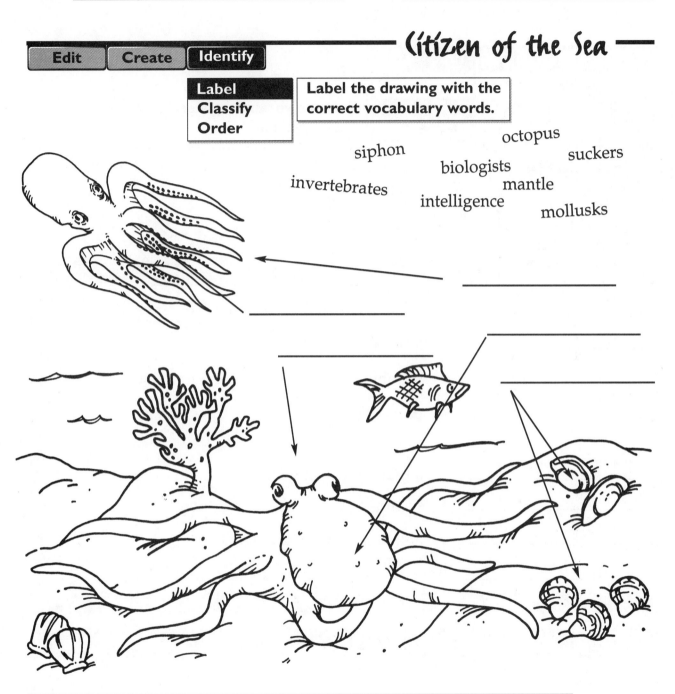

_____

_____

_____

_____

Also...

1. Explain what *biologists* do.
2. Find the antonym for *invertebrates*.
3. Tell which animal has the higher *intelligence*, a dolphin or a shark.

Name_____ Date _____

Identify
Find
Define

Find the vocabulary word that fits each meaning.

octopus
biologists

mantle

invertebrates

intelligence
siphon

suckers

mollusks

Underwater Explorer

_____ 1. the baglike area in back of the octopus' eyes

_____ 2. a sea animal with eight arms

_____ 3. the ability to think, learn, and understand

_____ 4. parts of an octopus' body by which it clings to things

_____ 5. a tube by which water is taken in or forced out

_____ 6. scientists who study living things

_____ 7. animals with hard shells

_____ 8. animals without backbones

Master of Disguise

Complete the outline.

_____

I. Cephalopods
  A. _____
    1. Parts of the body
      a. _____
      b. _____
      c. _____

Underwater Forest

Read this information about an unusual forest. Think about the meanings of the words in bold type.

Forests cover parts of every continent except Antarctica. These large tree-covered areas are teeming with life. Mammals, songbirds, insects, and wildflowers make their home in the tangle of greenery. Though you may find it hard to believe, there are also forests under the water. These forests are made of **seaweed**. The seaweed that makes up the underwater forest is called giant **kelp**. These plants grow in the cool coastal waters along the western coast of North America. Kelp forests also are found along the coasts of all the other continents. Even Antarctica has a kelp forest.

Giant kelp is one of the world's fastest growing plants. It can grow as much as 300 feet (100 meters) in a single year. That's as high as a 30-story building! When the plant reaches the surface, it spreads out and forms a floating mat.

The kelp plant has four parts. The part of the plant that is like a leaf is called the **blade**. Blades take in sunlight to make food. At the base of each blade is an air-filled bubble called the **float**. Floats help the plant bob up toward the sunlight. The stem-like part of the plant is called the **stipe**. The **holdfast**, which is like a root, anchors the plant to the ocean floor.

Like tree forests, a kelp forest is home to hundreds of different animals. Crabs, lobsters, octopuses, and sea stars cling to the rocky bottom. Shrimp, snail, jellyfish, and a variety of fish come to feed on the swaying plants. Sea birds roost on the floating mat at the water's surface.

Kelp forests are important, not only to animals, but to people. Farmers use kelp to **fertilize** their gardens. Because it's high in vitamins and minerals, kelp is an important food. Try it! You may like it.

Name_____ Date _____

| Edit | Create | **Identify** |

Label
Classify
Estimate

Label the drawing with the correct vocabulary words.

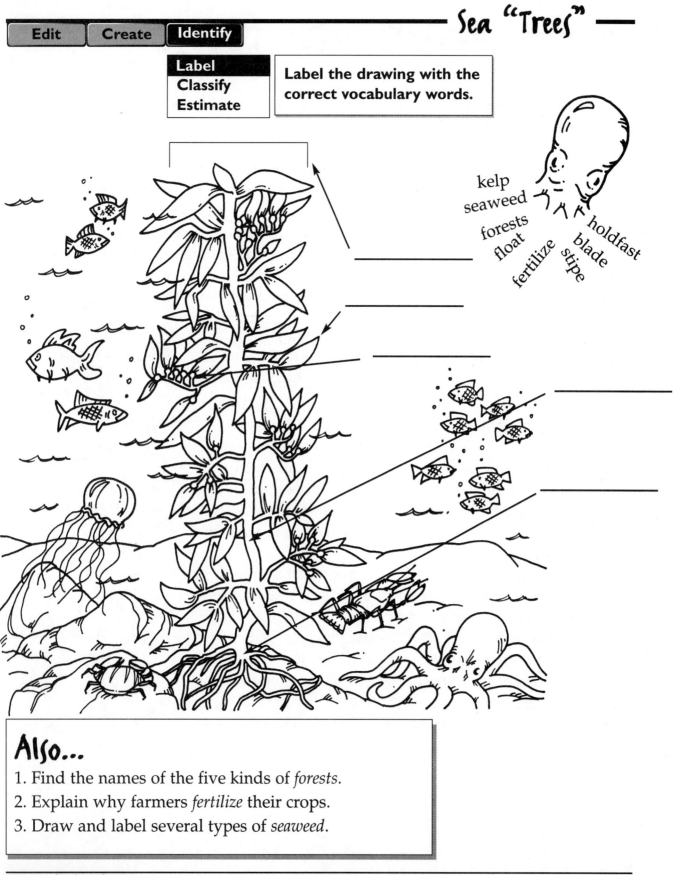

kelp
seaweed
forests
float
fertilize
stipe
blade
holdfast

_____

_____

_____

_____

Also...

1. Find the names of the five kinds of *forests*.
2. Explain why farmers *fertilize* their crops.
3. Draw and label several types of *seaweed*.

Research   Apply   **Process**

Find
Classify
Define

Find the vocabulary word
that fits each meaning.

blade
holdfast
kelp
seaweed
forests
stipe   float
fertilize

Sea "Trees"

ACROSS
2. air-filled bubble at the base of each blade
5. a plant that grows in the sea
6. a large, brown seaweed
7. dense growths of trees covering large areas of land
8. the "stem" of the kelp plant

DOWN
1. the "root" of the kelp plant
3. put something on the soil to make plants grow better
4. the "leaf" of the kelp plant

- Eek! There's a Bug in the House! -

Read this information about some insects. Think about the meanings of the words in bold type.

If you're interested in working as an **entomologist**—a person who studies insects—you don't have to make a special expedition to the Amazon rain forest or the Serengeti Plain. You can find an amazing number of bugs right in your own home. You can start your search in your bedroom. Your bed is full of **dust mites**. They eat the tiny flakes of skin that fall from your body. The flakes are so small they can pass through the weave in your pajamas and through your bed sheet where dust mites are waiting to feed.

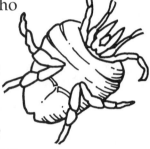

Now, go into your closet. If you find holes in a wool sweater, they were made by **clothes moths**. The female clothes moth likes a dry, warm, and dark place to lay her eggs. Your sweater was ideal. When the eggs hatched, **larvae**, or caterpillars, **emerged**. They fed on your sweater and made the holes.

Next, check the living room. Do you see small holes in your grandmother's table? They were made by a **furniture beetle**. This insect lays its eggs in cracks on the wood's surface. Once the larvae emerge from the eggs, they dig tunnels through the wood, eating as they go.

Finally, let's look in the kitchen. That noise you hear is made by the flapping wings of a **housefly**. Unlike the other insects you saw, this insect feeds on human food. It dissolves the food with chemicals that it passes down its **proboscis**, a long coiled tube. Then it sucks the soupy substance back up the proboscis into its mouth. Houseflies spread germs, so always keep your food covered.

Many other insects live in your home. They give birth, feed, reproduce, and die—all within your own four walls. Most never go outside. They don't have to! They're very comfortable inside.

Your Personal Zoo

Edit   **Create**   **Identify**

Label
Find
Order

Label the drawing with the
correct vocabulary words.

entomologist   clothes moths

larvae   emerged

furniture beetle

housefly   proboscis   dust mites

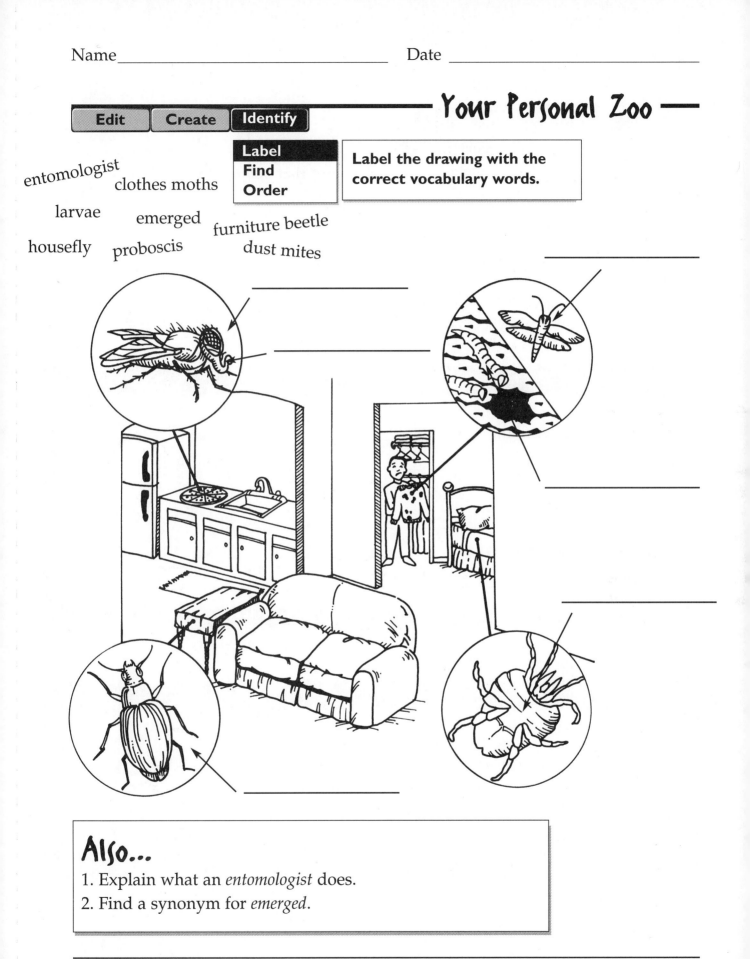

Also...

1. Explain what an *entomologist* does.
2. Find a synonym for *emerged*.

Research   Apply   **Process**

Classify
Identify
Match

Classify the vocabulary words. Write
the word that belongs in each group.

larvae housefly

dust mites

clothes moths

furniture beetle

emerged

entomologist

proboscis

House Guests

1. termite, carpenter ant, _____

2. wings, eyes, head, _____

3. biologist, zoologist, _____

4. fruit fly, bluebottle, _____

5. adult, eggs, pupa, caterpillar, _____

6. demodex mites, lice, _____

U

D

L   R

Wool Munchers

Make a chart showing the life cycle of a *clothes moth*.
Label the four stages: eggs, larvae or caterpillars,
pupae, and adults. Write a caption explaining what
happens in each stage. Use the word *emerged* in your
explanation.

U

L   R

——— Unit IV Review ———

Synonyms are words that have the same or almost the same meaning. Read these sentences. Circle the synonym for each vocabulary word in bold type.

fertilize   1. If you enrich the soil, you'll have a healthier crop.

emerged   2. A butterfly arose from the cocoon.

dissolve   3. To make pudding, evaporate the powder in milk.

mollusks   4. We cooked the lobsters and clams in large kettles.

kelp   5. Waves washed seaweed onto the shore.

proboscis   6. Some insects take in food through a tube.

evolved   7. Scientists think that birds developed from reptiles.

pollinate   8. Cranberry growers depend on bees to fertilize the plants.

siphon   9. Clams and squid take in water through a tube-like organ.

floats   10. Bubbles at the base of each blade help the kelp plant bob up toward the sunlight.

Unit IV Review

Choose a word from the Word List to complete the analogy.

Word List

endangered	seaweed	lobes	habitats	larvae
stipe	specimen	siphon	blade	holdfast
entomologists	invertebrates	kelp	mollusks	forests

11. <u>Animals</u> are to _____ as <u>people</u> are to <u>homes</u>.

12. <u>Stem</u> is to <u>rose</u> as _____ is to <u>kelp</u>.

13. <u>All</u> is to <u>species</u> as <u>one</u> is to _____.

14. _____ is to <u>trees</u> as <u>reefs</u> is to <u>coral</u>.

15. <u>Hands</u> are to <u>fingers</u> as <u>ears</u> are to _____.

16. <u>Octopi</u> are to _____ as <u>dogs</u> are to <u>vertebrates</u>.

17. <u>Sand</u> is to <u>grain</u> as <u>grass</u> is to _____.

18. _____ is to <u>kelp</u> as <u>root</u> is to <u>flower</u>.

19. <u>Chicks</u> are to <u>hens</u> as _____ are to <u>caterpillars</u>.

20. <u>Rocks</u> are to <u>geologists</u> as <u>insects</u> are to _____.

Name_____ Date _____

A Sport for Everyone

Read this information about backpacking. Think about the meanings of the words in bold type.

Stop and think! Where do you spend most of your time? You spend it in some kind of building—the school, your house or apartment building, stores, a church or temple. You work, watch TV, play video games, and sleep—all indoors. It's easy to forget, but there's a whole new world outside your door. The best way to explore it is to go **backpacking**.

Backpacking means to go hiking on foot. You bring only what you can carry on your back. Are you eager to get started? Wait a minute! Before you go anywhere, you should gather some basic **equipment**. First you need some **comfortable** shoes or boots. Never go out on the trial in sneakers or running shoes. They are not sturdy enough for most hiking, and they get wet too easily. Always carry a waterproof jacket or **poncho**, especially if you are hiking in a wet climate, or if the weather forecast calls for rain. Finally, you need a backpack or a **daypack**. Be sure it includes **adjustable** shoulder straps. It's also a good idea to have a compass, a leak-proof water bottle, and a map. If you plan to hike in a wilderness area, you can buy special maps called **topographic** maps that show the trails and mountains.

One-day hikes are the easiest to organize. Arrange a trip with a small group of friends. Remember! Hiking in a group is safer than hiking alone. Decide how far you will go. For most people, a distance of 10 to 12 miles (about 15 to 20 kilometers) is far enough in a day if they are already used to walking. Until you have gained some hiking experience, don't go into unfamiliar **territory** without taking along an experienced hiker.

Wherever you go, enjoy yourself. You may be tired when you get home, but you'll soon be planning another hike.

On the Trail

Edit **Create** **Identify**

Label
Order
Find

Label the drawing with the correct vocabulary words.

territory

poncho   backpacking   equipment

adjustable   comfortable   daypack

topographic

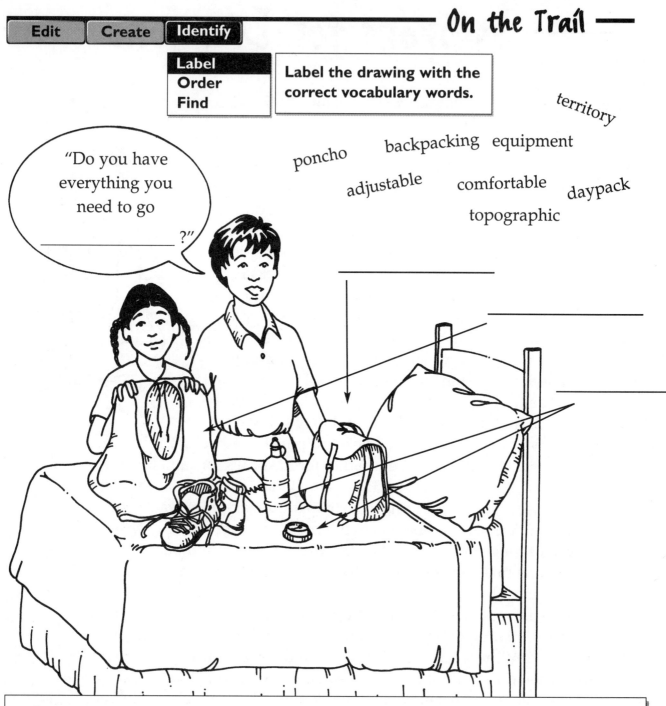

"Do you have everything you need to go _____?"

Also...

1. Demonstrate how a *daypack* or a backpack with *adjustable* shoulder straps works.
2. Find an antonym for *comfortable*.
3. Find a synonym for *territory*.
4. Draw a *topographic* map. Tell what information it contains.

Name_____ Date _____

Replace
Match
Find

Replace the word or words in bold type with a vocabulary word.

poncho

adjustable

equipment

daypack

territory

comfortable

topographic

backpacking

Hit the Road

1. My friends and I went **hiking on foot** in the park. _____

2. Sam borrowed some **gear** for the trip. _____

3. His boots were not **satisfactory**, however. _____

4. Fortunately, he had some tape in his **knapsack** and used it to bandage his blister. _____

5. When it started to rain, I put on my **cloak**. _____

6. The hood is **able to be changed**. _____

7. I plotted our route on a **showing the physical features of a place** map. _____

8. I was amazed that we covered so much **land area** in such a short time. _____

The Sporting Life

Write an ad for a daypack. Use the words *equipment*, *adjustable*, and *comfortable* in your ad. Be sure to illustrate it.

Let's Make a Deal!

**Read this information about collecting baseball cards.
Think about the meanings of the words in bold type.**

Four teenagers huddle in a corner. Each holds a handful of baseball cards. "I'll trade you a Luis Tiant for a Wade Boggs," one boy offers. Is this an even trade? Would you agree to it? You have to be fairly knowledgeable to be a **collector**.

How can you **estimate** the value of a card? First of all you look at the card's condition. Does it have minor **defects**, such as worn edges? Are the colors uneven? Does it have scratches or holes? Obviously, the better the card's condition, the more **valuable** it is. There are other **factors** to consider. One is what **economists** call the "law of supply and demand." When a lot of people want a certain card but not many copies are available, the card's value soars. A player's performance also affects the card's value. The cards of players with high batting averages are worth more than players whose careers are crashing.

As you can see, card collecting is serious business. Candy and gum companies began **distributing** baseball cards with pictures of the players included in the packs. Then someone had an idea. Why not print pictures of baseball players on the cardboard to **attract** customers? These early cards featured simple photographs or even drawings. Today manufacturing baseball cards has become a multi-million-dollar business.

You can start building your own set. Buy a few wax packs—small packs of cards—at a supermarket, drugstore, or bookstore near you. Then open the packs and see what you've got. After a while, you may find you have more than one copy of a single card. Those cards are valuable. You can trade them for the cards you need to complete a set. Building a set from scratch takes time, but it's also a lot more fun than just buying a complete set from a card dealer.

The Grand Slam Collection

Edit   Create   Identify

Label
Classify
Order

Label the drawing with the correct vocabulary words.

_____

collector
estimate
valuable   defects
factors   attract
economists
distributing

_____

When you try to _____ a card's value, you must consider several _____.

Also...

1. Draw some *valuable* items.
2. Name two famous *economists*. Explain what they do.
3. Find an antonym for *attract*.
4. Demonstrate the meaning of *distributing*.

Research   Apply   **Process**

Identify
Match
Find

**Identify the vocabulary word
that fits each meaning.**

factors

valuable   estimate   collector   defects

distributing   economists

attract

New Cards on the Block

conditions or details

					1	

giving out in shares

					7					3

to guess the cost of something

				5			4

to draw by exciting interest

				6		

a person who gathers something as a hobby

	2							

people who study how money and goods are produced

							8		

Write the numbered letters in the puzzle. You will discover
the name of a baseball player whose card is valuable.

1	2	3	4	1		5	6	1	7	8

O'er the Bounding Main

Read this information about sailing. Think about the meanings of the words in bold type.

Long ago, people traveled down rivers by straddling floating logs. Later, they hollowed out the log to make a place to sit. They used long poles to **propel** the log forward. Soon they were building boats by fashioning together wooden planks. They built larger and heavier boats. It took many rowers to move them. Then someone had an idea: Why not use the power of the wind to move the boat? So they attached a sail to it. The sail was probably made of animal skins.

Today most sailboats are made of fiberglass. Fiberglass boats are easier to care for than wooden boats and more affordable. As a result, sailing is becoming more and more popular. People sail all kinds of boats—from small sailboards to great cruising **yachts**. A small boat, however, is best for learning how to sail.

Before you set foot on a boat, you should know the names of the different parts of the boat. The body, or **hull**, of a sailboat is pointed in front and tapers off with a curve to the back. At the stern, or back, of the boat is the **rudder** that is used to steer the boat. Smaller boats have a **tiller** to turn the rudder; larger boats have a wheel. The **mast**, which is a tall pole, supports the sail. The **boom**, which is a somewhat shorter pole, supports the foot of the sail.

The two forces that move the boat ahead are the wind swirling past the sail on one side, and the pressure of water against the underwater **keel**, or centerboard, on the other side. Does this sound complicated? Fortunately, you don't have to understand how these forces work in order to sail a boat. All you have to do to get started sailing is to be aware of the direction the wind is blowing and set the sail. You'll be off on a great adventure!

Ahoy, Mateys!

| Edit | Create | **Identify** |

Label
Match
Estimate

Label each drawing with the
correct vocabulary words.

tiller   boom

hull

keel   mast

rudder   yachts

propel

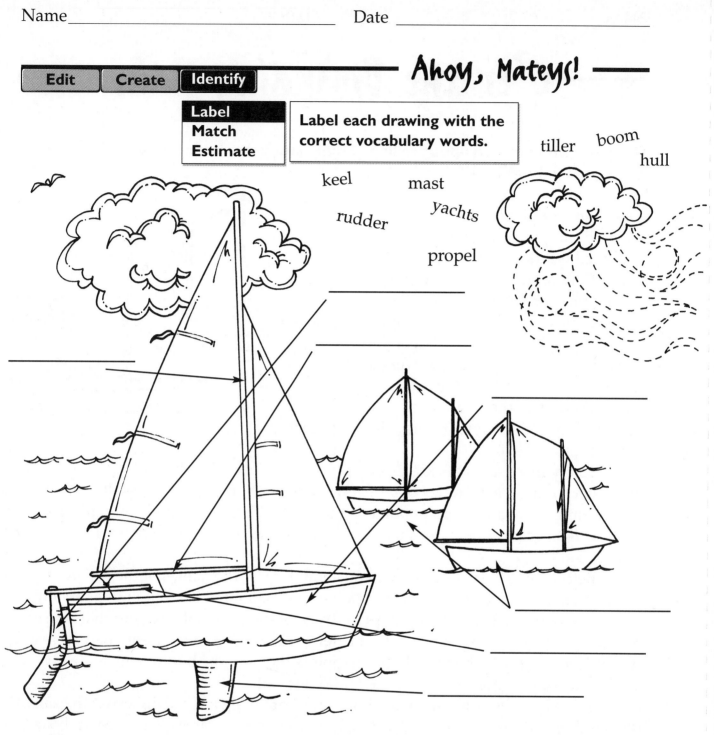

Also...

1. Find a synonym for *propel*.
2. Find photographs of some *yachts*. Explain the difference between
   a ketch and yawl.

Name_____ Date _____

| Research | Apply | **Process** |

Identify
Define
Find

tiller

mast   yachts

boom

keel   rudder   hull   propel

| **Find the vocabulary word that fits each meaning.** |

Ready About!

_____ 1. an upright pole that supports the sails

_____ 2. a movable board that is mounted at the rear of a boat

_____ 3. cause to move forward

_____ 4. a pole that supports the foot of a sail

_____ 5. small ships used for pleasure trips

_____ 6. a wooden or metal piece that runs along the center of the bottom of a boat

_____ 7. bar or handle used to turn a boat's rudder

_____ 8. the body of a boat

Hard Alee!

The shape of a keel varies from sailboat to sailboat. Find photographs or pictures of fin-keeled boats and full-keeled boats. Compare their shapes. Find out how the shape of the keel affects a boat's performance.

Name_____ Date _____

Tennis, Anyone?

Read this information about the game of tennis. Think about the meanings of the words in bold type.

Like many other sports, **tennis** is a very old game. Historians think that the ancient Egyptians, Greeks, and Romans played a game similar to tennis thousands of years ago. Lawn tennis used to be played on neatly manicured lawns, but grass courts are difficult and expensive to maintain. Today, the only major **tournament** played on grass is the All-England championships at Wimbledon.

As you can see from the diagram, a tennis court is a rectangular area 78 feet long and 36 feet wide. At each end of the playing area is a **baseline**. The lines that connect the baselines are called **sidelines**. The area between the two sidelines is called the **alley**. In the middle of the court is a three-foot-high net. On each side of the net are two **service courts**.

Other than a court, all you need to play tennis are a racquet, some tennis balls, and one or three other people, depending on which game you play. When two people play, the game is called singles. When four people play, it is called doubles. The players **rally,** or hit the ball back and forth over the net. The ball cannot bounce more than once before a player has to hit it back over the net.

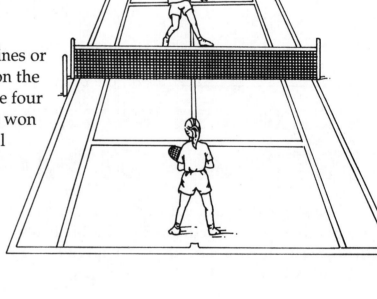

You score a point when your **opponent** hits the ball outside the lines or fails to return the ball over the net on the first bounce. The first player to score four points wins a game. After you have won six games, you've won a set. Several sets make up a match.

Like other sports, you need to practice in order to become a good tennis player. The more you practice, the better you'll get. Who knows, someday you may be good enough to play at Wimbledon!

Edit | Create | **Identify**

Getting Ready to Play

Label
Classify
Order

Label the drawing with the
correct vocabulary words.

opponent   rally   tennis
alley   tournament
sidelines
service courts   baseline

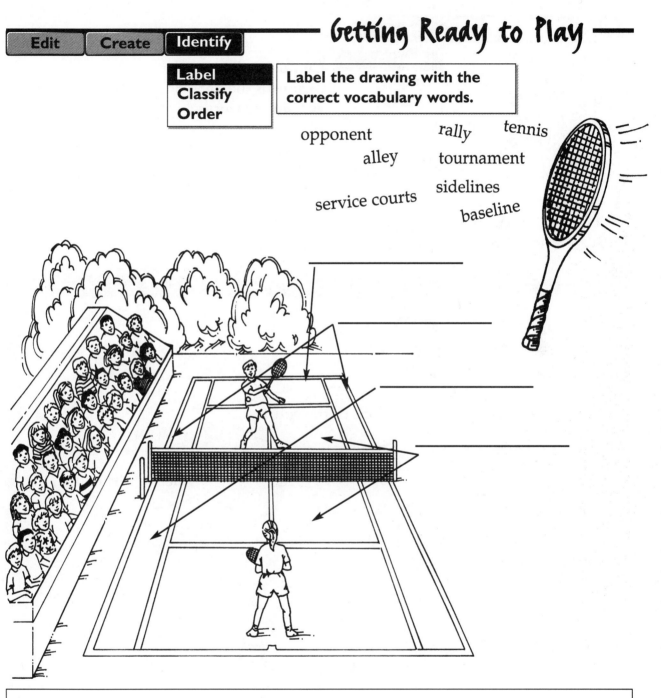

_____

_____

_____

_____

Also...

1. Name some *tennis* stars.
2. Find an antonym for *opponent*.
3. Describe the first kind of *tournament*.
4. Demonstrate the meaning of the word *rally*.

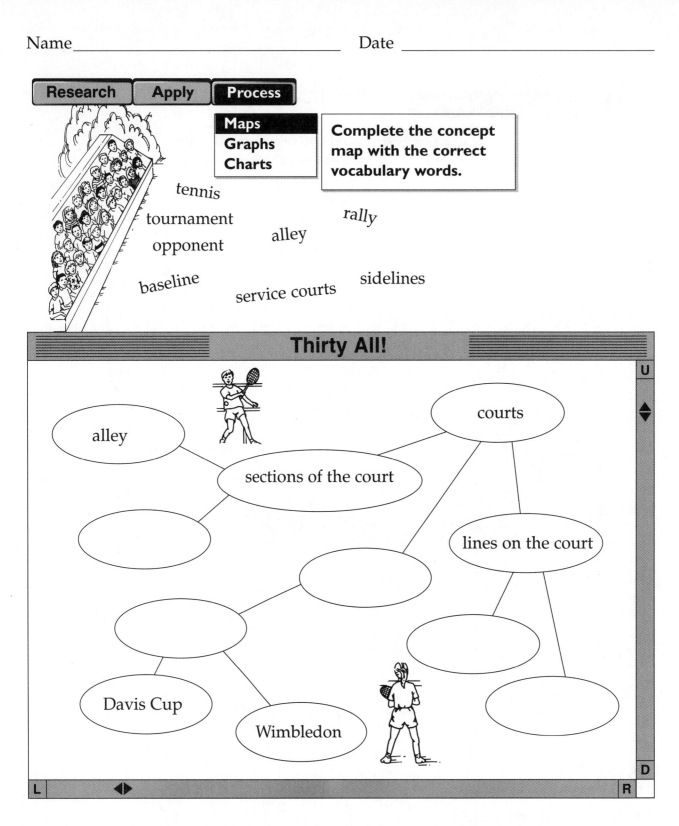

Research   Apply   Process

Maps
Graphs
Charts

Complete the concept
map with the correct
vocabulary words.

tennis

tournament   rally

opponent   alley

baseline

                service courts   sidelines

Thirty All!

alley

sections of the court

courts

lines on the court

Davis Cup

Wimbledon

Imagine you are a sports columnist for your school newspaper. Write
an article about a tennis match between two local champions. Use the
words *tennis*, *rally*, and *opponent* in your article. Be sure to include
information about who, what, where, when, and why.

—So . . . You Want to be a Gymnast!—

Read this information about gymnastics. Think about the meanings of the words in bold type.

Like millions of others around the world, you probably watch gymnastic events on television. You applaud as the athletes perform spectacular forward and backward **somersaults**. You hold your breath as they swing and circle around the **parallel bars** and do handstands on the **balance beam**. You may become so inspired by the acrobatic **feats** of the athletes that you say to yourself, "I want to be a gymnast!"

How do you become a **gymnast**? What basic skills do you need to succeed? What special qualities must you have? What equipment do you need? How do you find a good instructor? These are just a few of the questions you must answer if you are thinking of becoming involved with the sport.

The first step is to find a school that has **qualified** instructors that are experienced at all levels of coaching. Take your time choosing a school. Contact the U.S. Gymnastics Federation and your local recreation department.

As a beginner, you won't need much equipment. Girls wear leotards and gymnastics slippers, while boys wear gym shorts and T-shirts. As you progress, you will need handguards, wristbands, gymnastics shoes, and a uniform.

The exercises that you will perform call for balance, **agility**, and perfect control of the body. To become a top gymnast, you must go through a difficult training program to develop strong muscles, a supple body, and **stamina**. It's important, therefore, that you have healthy eating and sleeping habits.

Don't expect to become a Kurt Thomas or a Nadia Comaneci overnight. Being a gymnast takes practice, patience, and hard work. With proper instruction and a real effort on your part, you should be able to reach your goals.

Name_____ Date _____

| Edit | Create | **Identify** |

Label
Estimate
Match

Label the drawing with the correct vocabulary words.

qualified

balance beam

somersaults

parallel bars   feats

stamina

gymnast   agility

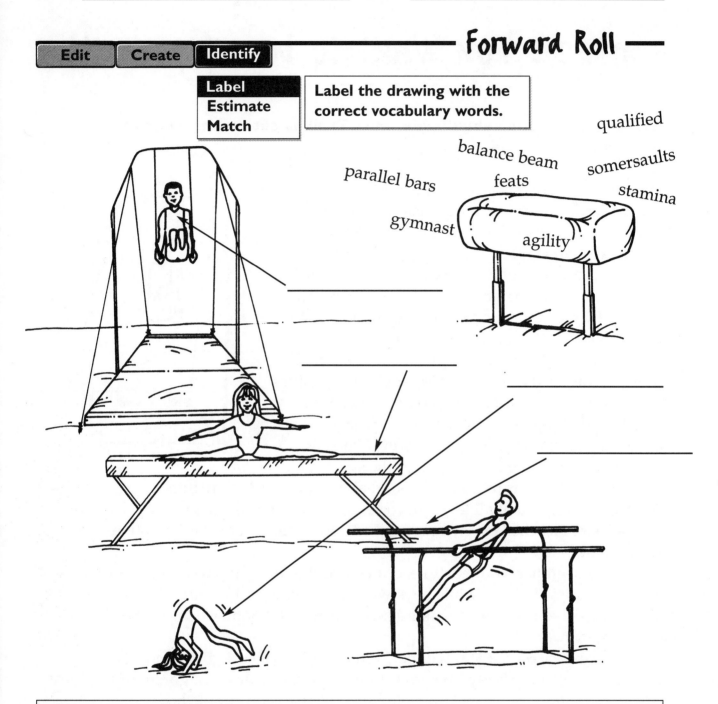

Also...

1. Find the names of some gymnastic *feats*.
2. Find a synonym for *qualified*.
3. Give an example of an activity a person with *stamina* can do.
4. Give an example of an activity a person with *agility* can do.

Name_____ Date _____

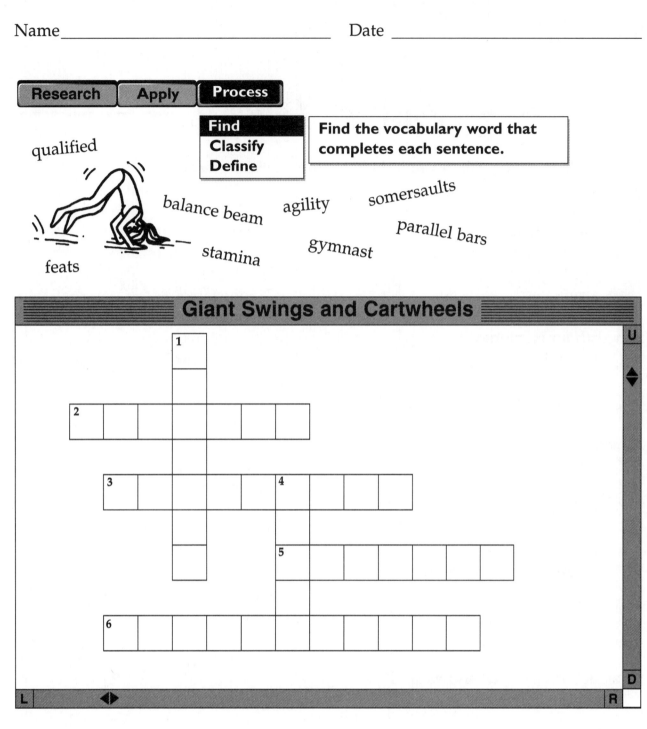

Research | Apply | **Process**

Find
Classify
Define

Find the vocabulary word that completes each sentence.

qualified

balance beam   agility   somersaults

parallel bars

stamina   gymnast

feats

Giant Swings and Cartwheels

ACROSS
2. Do you have the _____ to run 26 miles?
3. His years of experience _____ him to be the team's coach.
5. An acrobat must have _____ to be able to twist and turn.
6. The athlete performed forward and backward _____.

DOWN
1. Mary Lou Retton is a _____ who competed in the 1984 Olympics.
4. Climbing the mountain and crossing the stream were difficult _____ .

Unit V Review

Read each meaning. Fill in the bubble beside the word that fits the meaning.

1. an area of land
   ○ tournament
   ○ territory
   ○ atrium

2. worth much money
   ○ valuable
   ○ qualified
   ○ involuntary

3. cause to move forward
   ○ convert
   ○ locate
   ○ propel

4. a person who is against another in a fight, contest, or debate
   ○ opponent
   ○ gymnast
   ○ economist

5. an act or deed that shows skill, strength, or bravery
   ○ stamina
   ○ factor
   ○ feat

6. able to be changed or regulated so as to correct or improve
   ○ valuable
   ○ adjustable
   ○ comfortable

7. calculate roughly
   ○ rally
   ○ attract
   ○ estimate

8. a movable board that is mounted at the rear of a boat
   ○ rudder
   ○ keel
   ○ poncho

9. hit a ball back and forth over a net
   ○ somersault
   ○ rally
   ○ distribute

10. strength; endurance
    ○ stamina
    ○ agility
    ○ topographic

Name_____ Date _____

Unit V Review

Choose a word from the Word List to complete each analogy.

Word List

attract	defects	adjustable	equipment	tiller
economists	poncho	valuable	distributing	rally
sidelines	emerged	balance beam	yacht	comfortable

11. Perfume is to _____ as skunk is to repel.

12. Skyscraper is to building as _____ is to boat.

13. Sailboat is to _____ as car is to steering wheel.

14. Acrobat is to high wire as gymnast is to _____.

15. Baseball is to foul lines as tennis is to _____.

16. Mistakes are to _____ as perfection is to excellence.

17. Seismologists are to earthquakes as _____ are to economy.

18. Sweater is to cold as _____ is to wet.

19. Happy is to glad as cozy is to _____.

20. Came out is to _____ as went in is to entered.

Name_____ Date _____

Vocabulary List

abdomen	dissolves	kelp	range
absorb	distributing	lagoon	rigid
access	dust mites	landform	robotic
adapt	eardrum	landmass	root
adjustable	earthquake	larvae	rotating
agility	economists	lens	rudder
alley	emerged	lobes	sculptures
aloft	endangered	locate	seaweed
aorta	engraved	maintained	sensitive
aquanaut	entomologist	mantle	service courts
aquatic	epicenter	marsupials	sidelines
atmosphere	equipment	mast	siphon
atolls	eruptions	memorable	solar
atrium	estimate	meteorites	somersaults
attract	evolved	microbes	spasms
author card	exposed	missions	species
backpacking	factors	moist	specimen
balance beam	feats	molars	spectators
barrier reef	fertilize	mollusks	stamina
baseline	filaments	mooring mast	stipe
biologists	flammable	mountain	subject card
blade	float	naturalist	submersible
blood vessels	forests	normal	suckers
boom	fossil fuels	octopus	summary
canines	fringing reefs	opponent	summit
carbon dioxide	funnel	orbit	Surveyor
cardiac muscle	furniture beetle	organisms	symptoms
catalog	geologists	organs	tennis
chambers	gondola	pandas	tentacles
clothes moths	gravity	parallel bars	territory
collector	greenhouse	parasite	tether
collided	gymnast	photographs	tides
colonies	habitats	platform	tiller
comfortable	heat exhaustion	pollinate	title card
complex	helium	polyps	topographic
conditions	holdfast	poncho	tornado
conscious	housefly	portable	tournament
contract	hull	predators	transparent
convert	hydrogen	premolars	transportation
coral	hypothermia	probe	tsunami
crown	image	proboscis	valuable
damage	incisors	project	valves
daypack	inflating	propel	ventricle
defects	inhabitants	propeller	vibrations
deflate	intelligence	protective	vortex
dentin	intervals	publisher	wetas
descends	invertebrates	pulp	yachts
designer	inverted	pulse	
detect	invisible	qualified	
diameter	involuntary	rain forest	
dirigible	keel	rally	

Answer Key
Vocabulary Grade 5

P.6/7/8
Assessment Test
1. comfortable
2. collided
3. adapted
4. deflate
5. maintain
6. a predator
7. invertebrates
8. distributing
9. a symptom
10. summary
11. parasite
12. colony
13. exposed
14. coral
15. mission
16. larvae
17. yachts
18. agility
19. abdomen
20. catalog
21. valves
22. tournament
23. conscious
24. access
25. intelligence

P.11
symptoms
heat exhaustion
hypothermia
1. spasms
2. pulse
3. rigid

P.14
1. blood vessels
2. contract
3. atrium
4. ventricle
5. valves
6. aorta
7. involuntary
8. cardiac muscle

P.17
crown
premolars
dentin
root
molars
pulp
PUZZLE:
cementum

P.20
1. organs
2. eardrum
3. complex
4. vibrations
5. damage

P.23
1. locate
2. catalog
3. publisher
4. summary
5. access

P.24/25
Unit I Review
1. flexible
2. expands
3. crown
4. unusual
5. lose
6. unaware
7. intentional
8. simple
9. hardhearted
10. bar
11. damage
12. crown
13. convert
14. exhaustion
15. vibration
16. eardrum
17. organs
18. publisher
19. pulp
20. aorta

P.28
1. summit
2. inhabitants
3. range
4. mountain
5. landform
6. Geologists

P.31
1. fossil fuels
2. carbon dioxide
3. atmosphere
4. greenhouse
5. solar
6. absorb

P.34
ACROSS:
3. gravity
5. tides
6. eruptions
7. tsunami
8. earthquake
DOWN:
1. detect
2. epicenter
4. intervals

P.37
1. descends
2. diameter
3. moist
4. funnel
5. rotating
6. tornado

P.40
polyps
coral
lagoon
tentacles
colonies
fringing reefs
PUZZLE:
sting ray

P.41/42
Unit II Review
1. absorb
2. interval
3. summit
4. descended
5. lagoon
6. detect
7. inhabitants
8. A tornado
9. Atolls
10. invisible
11. Geologists
12. gravity
13. moist
14. vortex
15. colonies
16. tentacles
17. eruptions
18. solar
19. greenhouse
20. collided

P.45
1. Surveyor
2. meteorites
3. missions
4. microbes or
organisms
5. orbit
6. probe

P.48
1. sculptures
2. spectators
3. helium
4. chambers
5. inflating
6. tether
7. deflate
8. designer

P.51
ACROSS:
4. inverted
5. photographs
7. image
8. exposed
DOWN:
1. lens
2. project
3. engraved
6. portable

P.54
1. Hydrogen
2. propeller
3. gondola
4. dirigible
5. aloft
6. flammable

P.57
submersible
aquatic
transparent
memorable
platform
PUZZLE:
bamboo coral

Answer Key (cont.)
Vocabulary Grade 5

P.58/59
Unit III Review
1. aquanaut
2. lens
3. helium
4. transparent
5. dirigible
6. orbit
7. portable
8. spectators
9. aloft
10. microbes
11. hydrogen
12. missions
13. image
14. deflate
15. aquatic
16. inverted
17. chambers
18. memorable
19. probe
20. gondola

P.62
marsupials
wetas
predators
endangered
species
habitats

P.65
1. naturalist
2. lobes
3. rain forest
4. filaments
5. parasite

P.68
1. mantle
2. octopus
3. intelligence
4. suckers
5. siphon
6. biologists
7. mollusks
8. invertebrates

Master of
Disguise:
Mollusks
A. Octopus
a. mantle
b. siphon
c. suckers

P.71
ACROSS:
2. float
5. seaweed
6. kelp
7. forests
8. stipe
DOWN:
1. holdfast
3. fertilize
4. blade

P.74
1. furniture beetle
2. proboscis
3. entomologist
4. housefly
5. larvae
6. dust mites

P.75/76
Unit IV Review
1. enrich
2. arose
3. evaporate
4. lobsters and
   clams
5. seaweed
6. tube
7. developed
8. fertilize
9. tube-like organ
10. Bubbles
11. habitats
12. stipe
13. specimen
14. Forests
15. lobes
16. invertebrates
17. blade
18. Holdfast
19. larvae
20. entomologists

P.79
1. backpacking
2. equipment
3. comfortable
4. daypack
5. poncho
6. adjustable
7. topographic
8. territory

P.82
factors
distributing
estimate
attract
collector
economists
PUZZLE:
Roger Maris

P.85
1. mast
2. rudder
3. propel
4. boom
5. yachts
6. keel
7. tiller
8. hull

P.88
tennis:
courts:
sections of court:
alley
service courts
lines on the
court:
baseline
sidelines
tournaments:
Davis &
Wimbledon

P.91
ACROSS:
2. stamina
3. qualified
5. agility
6. somersaults
DOWN:
1. gymnast
4. feats

P.92/93
Unit V Review
1. territory
2. valuable
3. propel
4. opponent
5. feat
6. adjustable
7. estimate
8. rudder
9. rally
10. stamina
11. attract
12. yacht
13. tiller
14. balance beam
15. sidelines
16. defects
17. economists
18. poncho
19. comfortable
20. emerged